The Story of Sugar

(Sara Ware Bassett)

CONTENTS

CHAPTER I

COLVERSHAM

"Oh, say, Bobbie, quit that algebra and come on out! You've stuck at it a full hour already. What's the use of cramming any more? You'll get through the exam all right; you know you always do," protested Van Blake as he flipped a scrap of blotting paper across the study table at his roommate.

Bob Carlton looked up from his book. "Perhaps you're right, Van," he replied, "but you see I can't be too sure on this stuff. Math isn't my strong point, and I simply must not fall down on it; if I should flunk it would break my father all up."

"You flunk! I'd like to see you doing it." Van smiled derisively. "When you fall down on an exam the rest of us better give up. You know perfectly well you'll get by. You are always worrying your head off when there's no earthly need of it. Now look at me. If there is any worrying to be done I'm the one that ought to be doing it. Do I look fussed? You don't catch your uncle losing any sleep over his exams--and yet I generally manage to scrape along, too."

"I know you do--you old eel!" Bob glanced admiringly at his friend. "I believe you just wriggle by on the strength of your grin."

"Well, if you are such a believer in a grin why don't you cultivate one yourself and see how far it will carry you?" chuckled Van. "The trouble with you, Bobbie, is your conscience; you ought to be operated on for it. Why are you so afraid you won't get good marks all the time?"

"I'm not afraid; but I'd be ashamed if I didn't," was the serious reply. "I promised my father that if he'd let me come to Colversham to school I'd do my best, and I mean to. It costs a pile of money for him to send me here, and it's only decent of me to hold up my end of the bargain."

Van Cortlandt Blake stretched his arms and gazed thoughtfully down at the ruler he was twirling in his fingers.

"Bobbie, you're a trump; I wish more fellows were like you. The difference between us is that while I perfectly agree with you I sit back and talk about it; you go ahead and do something. It's rotten of me not to work harder down here. I know my father is sore on it, and every time he writes I mean to take a brace and do better--honest I do, no kidding. But you know how it goes. Somebody wants me on the ball nine, or on the hockey team, or in the next play, and I say yes to every one of them. The first I know I haven't a minute to study and then I get ragged on the exams.

"You are too popular for your own good, Van. No, I'm not throwing spinach, straight I'm not. What I mean is that everybody likes you. Why, there isn't a more popular boy in the school! That's why you get pulled into every sort of thing that's going. It's all right, too, only if you expect to study any you've got to rise up in your boots and take a stand. That's why I shut myself up and grind regularly part of every evening. I don't enjoy doing it, but it's the only way."

Van rose and began to roam round the room uneasily.

"Goodness knows, Bobbie, if one of us didn't grind neither of us would get anywhere. By the way, did you manage to dig out that Caesar for to-morrow? Fire away and give me the product of your mighty brain. I guess I can memorize the translation if you read it to me enough times."

Bob did not reply.

"Well?"

"I don't think it is a straight thing for me to translate your Latin for you every day, Van," he said at last. "You ought not to ask me to do it."

"I know it; it's mighty low down--I acknowledge that," answered Van frankly. "But what would you have me do? Flunk it? Come on. I'll get it myself next time."

"That's what you always say, Van, but you never do."

"But I tell you I will. This week I've been so rushed with the Glee Club rehearsals I couldn't do a thing. But you wait and view yours truly next week."

Reluctantly Bob took up his Caesar and opened it.

"That's a gentleman, Bobbie. Some time when you're drowning I'll throw a plank to you. I knew you'd save my life."

"I do not approve of doing it at all," Bob observed, still searching for the place in the much worn brown text-book. "I've done about all your studying this term."

"I own it, oh Benefactor. Are you not my brain--my intellectual machinery? Could I live a day without you?"

Leaning across the table Van affectionately rumpled up Bob's tidy locks until every individual hair stood on end.

"If it weren't for me you'd be dropped back into the next class--that's what would happen to you; and you deserve it, too."

Van was silent.

"I know it. I haven't put in an hour of solid work for a month, Bob I ought to be ashamed, and I am." He paused. "But there's no use jumping all over myself if I haven't," he resumed, shifting to a more sprightly tone. "I've said I was going to take a spurt soon and I mean it. I'll begin next week."

"Why not start to-day?"

There was a rap at the door.

"Why not?" echoed Van, moving toward the door with evident relief. "Don't you see I can't? Somebody's always breaking in on my work. Here's somebody this very minute."

He flung open the door.

"Mail. A parcels-post package for you, Bob. I'll bet it's eats. Your mother's a corker at sending you things; I wish my mother sent me something now and then."

"Well, it's a little different with you. Your family live so far out west they can't very well mail grub to you; but Mater is right here in New York, and of course as she's near by she'd be no sort of a mother if she didn't send me something beside this prison fare. Come on and see what it is this time."

Bob loosened the string from the big box and began unwinding the wrappings.

"Plum-cake!" he cried. "A dandy great loaf! And here's olives, and preserved ginger, and sweet chocolate. She's put in salted almonds, too; and look--here's a tin box of Hannah's molasses cookies, the kind I used to like when I was a kid. Isn't my mother a peach?"

"She sure is; and she must think a lot of you," said Van slowly. "I wish my mother'd ever--"

"Maybe if you pitched in a little harder here she'd feel--"

"Oh, cut out the preaching, Bobbie," was the impatient retort. "I've had enough for one day."

Bob did not speak, but tore open the letter that had come with the bundle.

"Oh, listen to this, Van," he shouted excitedly. "Mother says they have decided to open the New Hampshire house for Easter. They're going up for my spring vacation and take in the sugaring off. What a lark! And listen to this. She writes: 'You'd better arrange to bring your roommate home with you for the holiday unless he has other plans.'"

"Oh, I say!"

"Could you go, Van?"

Bob eyed his chum eagerly.

"I don't see why I couldn't. I'm not going home to Colorado. It's too far. I was thinking of going to Boston with Ted Talbot, but I'd a good sight rather go batting with you, Bobbie, old man. It was fine of your mother to ask me. Where is the place?"

"Our farm? It's in Allenville, New Hampshire, near Mount Monadnock. It used to be my grandfather's home, and after he died and we all moved to New York Father fixed it over and kept it so we could go there summers. I've never been up in the spring, though. It will be no end of fun."

"I hope you do not call this weather spring," put in Van, sarcastically, pointing to the snow-buried hills outside.

"Well, it is the middle of March, and it ought to be spring, if it isn't," answered Bob. "Just think! Only a week more of cramming; then the exams, and we're off. I'm awfully glad you can go."

"You speak pretty cheerfully of the exams. I don't suppose you dread them much." Van lapsed into a moody silence, kicking the crumpled wrapping-paper into the fireplace. "You don't need to worry, Bob. But look at me. I'll be lucky if I squeak through at all. Of course I've never really flunked, but I've been so on the ragged edge of going under so many times that it's no fun."

"Cheer up! You'll get through. Why, man alive, you've got to. Now come on and get at this Latin and afterward we'll pitch into the plum-cake."

"What do you say we pitch into the cake first?"

"No, sir. Not a bite of cake will you get until you have done your Caesar. Come on, Van, like a good kid, and have it over; then we'll eat and talk about Allenville."

Once more Bob opened the book.

"Here we are! You've got to do it, Van, and to-morrow you'll be glad that you did. Stop fooling with that paper and bring your chair round this side of the desk. Begin here: _Cum Caesar esset_--"

Persistently Bob followed each line of the lesson down the page, translating and explaining as he went, and ungraciously Van Blake listened.

The little brass clock on the mantelpiece ticked noisily, and the late afternoon sun that streamed in through the windows lighted into scarlet the crimson wall-paper and threw into prominence the posters tacked upon it. It was a cozy room with its deep rattan chairs and pillow-strewn couch. Snow-shoes, fencing foils, boxing-gloves, and tennis racquets littered the corners, and on every side a general air of boyish untidiness prevailed.

Although the apartment was not, perhaps, as luxurious as a college room, it was nevertheless entirely comfortable, for the Colversham School boasted among its members not only boys of moderate means but the sons of some of the richest families in the country. It aimed to be a democratic institution, and in so far as this was possible it was; the school, however, was richly endowed and therefore its every appointment from its perfectly rolled tennis courts to its instructors and the Gothic architecture of its buildings was of the best.

Van Cortlandt Blake, whose father was a western manufacturer, had by pure chance stumbled upon Bob Carlton the day the two had alighted from the train and stood helpless among the new boys on the station platform, awaiting the motor-car which was to meet them and carry them up to the school. Before the five mile ride was finished and the automobile had turned into the avenue of Colversham the boys had agreed to room together. Bob came from New York City. He was younger than Van, slender, dark, and very much in earnest; he might even have passed for a grind had it not been for his sense of humor and his love for skating and tennis. As it was he proved to be a master at hockey, as the school team soon discovered, and before he had been a week at Colversham his classmates also found that he was most loyal in his friendships and a lad of unusual generosity.

Van Blake was of an entirely different type. Big, husky, happy-go-lucky--a poor student but a right jolly companion; a fellow who could pitch into any kind of sport and play an uncommonly good game at almost anything. More than that, he could rattle off ragtime untiringly and his nimble fingers could catch up on the piano any tune he heard whistled. What wonder he speedily became the idol of Colversham? He was a born leader, tactfully marshaling at will the boys who were his own age, and good-naturedly bullying those who were younger.

To the school authorities he presented a problem. His influence was strong and, they felt, not always good; yet there was not a teacher on the premises who did not like him. Intellectually they were forced to own that he was demoralizing. He was, moreover, a disturber of the social order. But his pranks were, after all, pure mischief and never malicious or underhanded. With a boy like Bob Carlton as a roommate and drag anchor the principal argued he could not go far astray.

And so the first year had passed without mishap, and already the second was nearing its close. The school board congratulated itself. Had the faculty known that for most of his scholarship, poor as it often was, Van Blake was indebted to the sheer will power of Bob Carlton they might have felt less sanguine. Day after day Bob had patiently tutored his big chum in order that he might contrive to scrape through his lessons. It was Bob who did the work and Van who serenely accepted the fruits of it--accepted it but too frequently with scant thanks and even with grumbling. Bob, however, doggedly kept at his self-imposed task. To-day's Latin translation was but an illustration of the daily program; Bob did the pioneering and Van came upon the field when the path was cleared of difficulties. And yet it was a glance of genuine affection that Bob cast at his friend stretched so comfortably in the big Morris chair with a pillow at his back.

"There, you lazy villain, I think you'll do!" he declared at last. "Don't forget about the hostages in the second line; you seem pretty shaky on that. I guess, though, you'll pull through alive."

"Bobbie, you're my guiding angel," returned the elder boy yawning. "When I make my pile and die rich I'm going to leave you all my money."

"Great Hat! Hear him. Leave me your money! What do you suppose I'm going to be doing while you're rolling up your millions? I intend to be rich myself, thank you," retorted Bob, throwing down his book. "Now for the plum-cake! You deserve about half the loaf, old man, but I shan't give it to you, for it would make you sick as a dog, and then I'd have you to take care of. Oh, I say, listen a minute! Isn't that the crowd coming from the gym? Open the window and whistle to them. Tell 'em to pile up here for a feed. And get your muscle to work on this olive bottle, Van. I can't get the cork out."

CHAPTER II

A NARROW ESCAPE

The dreaded examinations came and went and, as Van Blake expressed it, were passed with honor by Bobbie and with dishonor by himself. After the last one was over it was with a breath of relief that the two lads tossed pajamas and fresh linen into their suit-cases; collected snow-shoes and sweaters; and set out on their New Hampshire visit.

It had been a late spring and therefore although the buds were swelling and a few pussy-willows venturing from their houses the country was still in the grip of winter; great drifts buried roadside and valley and continued to obstruct those highways where travel was infrequent.

"There certainly is nothing very summerish about this New England weather of yours, Bob," remarked Van, as, on alighting from the train at Allenville, he buttoned closer his raccoon coat and stepped into the waiting sleigh which had come to meet them.

"The State did not realize you were coming, old man; otherwise they would have had some weather especially prepared for your benefit," Bob replied, springing into the sleigh beside his chum. "My, but this is a jolly old pung! Hear it creak. I say," he leaned forward to address the driver, "where did my father get this heirloom, David?"

"Law, Mr. Bob, this ain't your father's," David drawled. "He ain't got anything but wheeled vehicles in the barn, and not one of 'em will be a mite of use till April. I borrowed this turnout of the McMasters', who live a piece down the road; the foreman, you know. It was either this or a straight sledge, and we happened to be using the sledges collecting sap."

"Are you sugaring off already?" questioned Bob with evident disappointment. "I understood Father to say we'd get here in time to be in on that."

"Bless your soul, Mr. Bob, you'll see all you want of it," was David's quick answer. "There's gallons of sap that hasn't been boiled down yet. It's a great year for maple-sugar, a great year."

"Are some years better than others?" Van inquired.

"Yes, indeed. What you want to make the sap run is a good cold snap, followed by a thaw. That's just what we've been having. It's a prime combination."

He jerked the reins impatiently.

"Get up there, Admiral! He's the very worst horse to stop that ever was made. You see in summer he drags a hay-cart, and he has to keep halting for the hay to be piled on; then in the fall we use him for working on the road, and he has to wait while we pick up stones and spread gravel; in the spring he makes the rounds of the sugar orchard every morning and stands round on three legs while we empty the sap buckets into the cask on the sledge. Poor soul, he never seems to get going that he ain't hauled up. He's so used to it now that he'd rather stop than go, I reckon."

David's prophecy appeared to be quite true, for the Admiral proved to be so loath to proceed that every few paces he would hesitate, turn his head, and seem to be inquiring where the hay, stones, or sap buckets were to-day. It was only David's repeated urging which kept him moving at all. In consequence it was dark before the boys caught sight of the "Pine Ridge" lights gleaming through the tangle of hemlock boughs that screened the drive, and saw the door of the hospitable old farmhouse swing open.

"Well, I'll wager you're pretty hungry," a cheery voice called.

"Hungry, Mother! We're starved--hollow down to our shoe-strings!" Swinging himself out upon the steps Bob bent and kissed his mother. "Mother, this is my roommate, Van Blake," he added.

"I'm very glad to see you, Van," Mrs. Carlton said, putting both her hands into those of the big fellow who smiled down at her. "How strange it is that although you and Bob are such friends and he is continually talking and writing of you that you and I should never have met!"

"I don't just know how it's happened, Mrs. Carlton," Van answered. "It seems as if the times you've been at the school to visit I've either been away or shut up in the infirmary with chicken-pox or something. I'm great at catching diseases, you know--I get everything that's going. Father says he thinks I can't bear to let anything get by me."

He laughed boyishly.

"Speaking of fathers, where's Dad, Mater?"

"He stopped to put another log on the fire. Come in and see what a blaze we have ready for you."

The two boys followed her into the hall, while David staggered at the rear of the procession with the luggage.

Mr. Carlton came forward.

"This is Van Blake, Father," Bob said, proudly introducing his chum.

"I'm glad to see you, young man," Mr. Carlton responded. "Bob's friends will always find a welcome from us."

"Thank you, sir."

Mr. Carlton reflected a moment then asked abruptly:

"I don't suppose you happen to be a connection of the Colorado Blakes."

"I come from Colorado," replied Van quickly.

"You're not one of the sugar Blakes; not Asa Blake's son."

"Yes," cried Van. "Mr. Asa Blake is my father, and he is in the beet sugar business. Do you know him?"

"I believe I've met him," Mr. Carlton admitted hurriedly, stooping to push the glowing back-log a little further forward.

"Why, Father--"

Bob was interrupted.

"Come, boys," said Mrs. Carlton bustling in. "I guess you've warmed your fingers by this time. Bob, take Van up-stairs and tumble out of those fur coats as fast as ever you can so to be ready for dinner."

The lads needed no second bidding. They were up-stairs and back in the dining-room in a twinkling, and so eagerly did they chatter of their plans for the morrow that hungry though they were they almost forgot to eat.

"There are so many things to do that it is hard to decide where to begin," declared Bob. "Of course we want some coasting and some snow-shoeing; and we must climb Monadnock. Van says he hasn't seen a real mountain since he came East. Then we want to be on hand for the maple-sugar making. Why, ten days won't be half long enough to do everything we ought to do."

His mother laughed.

"You must have a good sleigh ride, too," she put in.

"I draw the line on a sleigh ride if we have to go with that horse that brought us up from the station," announced Bob.

"Me, too!" Van echoed.

"It would take you the entire ten days to get anywhere and back if you went sleighing with the Admiral," said Mr. Carlton.

Every one smiled.

"I'd advise your seizing upon the first clear day for your Monadnock tramp," Mr. Carlton continued. "You'd better make sure of good weather when you get it. It won't make so much difference with your other plans; but for the mountain trip you must have a good day."

"I do want Van to get the view from the top if he makes the climb," Bob answered.

So the chat went merrily on.

Yet despite the gaiety of the evening and Mr. Carlton's evident interest in the boys' holiday schemes Bob more than once caught his father furtively studying Van's profile. Obviously something either puzzled or annoyed him. There was, however, no want of cordiality in his hearty goodnight or in the zest with which he advocated that if the next morning proved to be unclouded the two lads better make certain of their mountain excursion. He even helped lay out the walk and offered many helpful suggestions. Bob's uneasiness lest his father should not like his chum vanished, and when he dropped into bed the last vague misgiving took flight, and he fell into a slumber so profound that morning came only too soon.

It was David who, entering softly to start the fire in the bedroom fireplace, awakened Bob.

He sat up and rubbed his eyes sleepily.

"What sort of a day is it, David?" he questioned in a whisper that he might not arouse Van, who was lying motionless beside him.

"It's a grand day, Mr. Bob. There ain't a cobweb in the sky."

David tiptoed out and Bob nestled down once more beneath the blankets. It was fun to lie there watching the logs blaze up and see your breath rise on the chilly air; it was fun, too, to know that no gong would sound as it did at school and compel you to rush madly into your clothes lest you be late for breakfast and chapel, and receive a black mark in consequence. No, for ten delicious days there was to be no such thing as hurry. Bob lay very still luxuriating in the thought. Then he glanced at Van, who was still immovable, his arm beneath his cheek. His friend's obliviousness to the world was irresistible. Bob raised himself carefully; caught up his pillow; took accurate aim; and let it fly.

It struck Van in the head, routing further possibility of sleep.

"Can't you let a fellow alone?" he snapped.

"Wake up, you old mummy!" shouted Bob. "A great mountain climber you are, sleeping here all day. Have you forgotten you're going up Monadnock to-day?"

"Hang Monadnock! I was sound asleep when you lammed that pillow at me, you heathen. What's the good of waking me up at this unearthly hour?" yawned Van.

"It's seven o'clock."

"Seven o'clock!" Van straightened up and stared. "Why, man alive, I haven't been asleep fifteen minutes."

"You've been lying like a log for nine mortal hours," chuckled Bob.

"Great Scott! Some sleep, isn't it? That's better than I do at Colversham."

"Rat_her!_"

"Well, I need sleep. I'm worn out with over-study."

"You are, like--"

"I am. I'm an intellectual wreck," moaned Van. "It's the Latin."

Bob burst into a shout, which was cut short by a rap at the door.

"Time to get up, boys," called the cheery voice of Mr. Carlton. "Step lively, please. Here's a can of hot water."

The boys wasted no more time in fooling.

They bathed, dressed, and almost before they knew it were at the table partaking of a hearty breakfast which was capped by heaps of golden brown pancakes rendered even more golden by the sea of maple-syrup in which they floated.

"I'll never be able to climb anything after this meal," Van gasped as he left the table and was thrusting his arms into his sweater.

Bob grinned.

"Don't expect us back before late afternoon, Father," he called over his shoulder. "We've a long slow climb ahead of us because of the snow. Probably we shall find it drifted in lots of places. Then we shall want some time at the top of the mountain, you know. Besides, we're going to stop and cook chops, and that will delay us. So don't worry if we don't turn up much before dinner time."

"You're sure you know the trail, Bob?" his mother called as the trampers went down the steps.

"Why, Mother dear, what a question! Know the trail? Haven't I climbed that mountain so many times that I could go up it backwards and with my eyes shut?"

"I guess that's true, Mother," agreed Mr. Carlton reassuringly.

"Good-bye, then," said Bob's mother. "Have a fine day and don't freeze your noses."

The boys waved, and with a scuff of their snow-shoes were off.

The climb was indeed a stiff one. At first the trail led through low, flat woods, fragrant with hemlock and balsam; here it was sheltered and warm. But soon the real ascent began.

"We follow the bed of this brook almost to the top," explained Bob who was leading the way. "We come into it here, you see. In summer it is a narrow path clearly marked by rough stones; you wouldn't believe how different it looks now all covered with snow. It doesn't seem like the same place. I didn't realize what a difference the snow would make in everything. But, anyway, we can't miss the way with these great boulders along the sides of the path; and even if we did the trees are blazed."

They pushed on for some time.

Then the strap of Van's snow-shoe broke.

"Oh, thunder! Got a knife, Bob?" he called. "This darn thing's busted. I'll have to haul to for repairs."

Bob stopped impatiently.

"Why didn't you look at it before you started?" he said.

"Never thought of it, Old Preparedness," was the good-natured reply. "No matter, I have some string and I think I can fix it."

It took some time, however, to make the fastening to the shoe and moccasin secure, and in the meantime the sun went behind a cloud.

"I guess Father wasn't a very good weather prophet," remarked Bob, glancing at the sky. "It seems to be clouding up."

"Don't fret. What do we care?" was Van's easy answer. "We're not really after the view. I don't give a hurrah for what we see when we get to the top; what I want is the fun of doing it."

They shuffled on.

"I'll be glad when this luncheon is inside instead of outside of me, won't you?"

puffed Bob. "It's almighty heavy to carry."

"It isn't the lunch I mind. It's all these infernal clothes," was Van's retort. "I don't see what on earth I wore so many things for."

"You'll want them by and by."

"I bet I won't!" protested Van. "I'm going to tie my red sweater to this tree and leave it here; I can't be bothered with so much stuff."

"You'll be cold when you get to the top."

"No, I won't. And anyway I'd rather be too cold then than too hot now. One's no better than the other."

Deaf to Bob's counsel Van resolutely wound the offending sweater about a great white birch tree that stood at a fork of the path.

"You'll be sorry," was Bob's parting thrust as they plodded on.

The trail was now steep and so narrow that frequently Bob had to stop and search for the blazing on the trees.

"Of course I know my way, all right," he insisted. "Still, it is mighty different in winter from what it is at other seasons of the year, I'll admit that. Remember, I've never climbed this hill when the snow was on the ground. However, when we once get to the top the coming down will be a cinch, because we can follow our own tracks."

It was nearly two o'clock before the boys reached the top of the mountain. Over the landscape hung a mass of heavy gray clouds beneath which the sun was hidden; the wind was cutting as a knife, and while Van sought the shelter of an old shack Bob roamed about, delighting in the familiar scene.

"Why don't you come over here and look at the view?" he called to his companion. "It is fairly clear in spite of the clouds."

Van shivered.

"Oh, I don't want to. I don't care a hang for the view--I told you that before. I'm just hungry. Let's get a fire going and cook the chops. What do you say?"

"You're cold. I said you would be."

"I'm not. I'm starved, though. Where can we get some wood?"

Bob glanced about.

"There seems to be plenty of undergrowth down in that hollow. Take my knife and cut away some of it. There's a piece of an old stump, too, that ought to burn well if it isn't too wet."

"That thing would never burn; but the brush will. Sling me the knife and I'll cut an armful. Let's build it in that little rocky shelter. Thanks to my camping training I'm right at home on this job."

Van's boast was no idle one. Soon the fire was crackling merrily and the chops and bacon were sizzling in the frying-pan. Bob unpacked the sandwiches and the thermos bottle of hot chocolate.

It was a regal luncheon.

How good everything tasted!

"I believe I was cold," Van admitted, rubbing his hands over the dying embers of the blaze. "But I'm warm as toast now. Is there any more grub left to eat?"

"Not a crumb--why? Are you still hungry?" queried Bob who was packing up the camping kit.

Van chuckled.

"Well, not exactly. I only thought we ought not to waste anything."

Bob glanced up and laughed; then his face grew sober.

"I say, there's a snowflake!" he cried. "And another! Jove, Van, it's begun to snow!"

"We better be getting down, I suppose," drawled Van.

"Just that, old man; fast as we can, too. Come on."

"What's your hurry? It will be a lark."

"It will be no lark if it snows much--I'll tell you that," replied Bob seriously. "Besides, the folks will worry. Come ahead."

They turned back down the trail.

The snowfall increased.

"You can hardly see our tracks already," Bob called over his shoulder. "And this wind is fierce. I had no idea it would snow. It is awfully wet and sticky snow, too; see how it clings to the trees."

They sped on.

The descent was far easier than the climb, and they could go quickly.

"I don't remember that big rock," exclaimed Van suddenly, pointing to a huge boulder that fronted them. "Isn't it a whacker! Odd that I didn't notice it when we came up. Could we have passed it and not seen it?"

[Illustration: "I DON'T REMEMBER THAT BIG ROCK"]

"I suppose we must have," Bob answered. "I don't remember it, though. Everything looks queer and different in the storm. It's a regular squall. How quickly it came!"

"Can you still see our tracks?"

"No. But of course we're right; I couldn't miss my way after coming over this path so many times."

"Can you see the blazes on the trees?"

"No, silly. How could I when they are all plastered over thick with snow?" was Bob's scornful retort. He was silent for a moment. "But don't you worry," he declared. "I am certain we came this way--at least I *think* we did."

His tone, however, was less convincing.

They went on.

"We don't seem to be coming out anywhere, do we?" Van finally asked.

"No."

"Didn't we pass a little clearing somewhere on the way up?"

"Yes, there was one."

"Have we passed it?"

"No."

"Then it's ahead of us."

"It ought to be. I say, suppose we stop a minute and brush the snow off these trees so to make sure we really are on the trail."

"A bully idea!"

The boys put down their packs and reconnoitred.

"There don't seem to be any marks on these trees," Van asserted after an interval of search.

"But there must be."

"Find them then--if you can."

Bob nervously scrutinized several gnarled trunks.

"You're right, Van," he owned at last. "We're off the trail; missed it somehow. We'd better go back; we can't be far wrong. Or better yet, you wait here while I hunt."

Bob was very grave.

"You bet I'm not going to be left here to be buried in snow like the Babes in the

Wood," protested Van gaily. "No sir-ee! I don't stay here. I'll help hunt for the path too. Now don't go getting nervous, Bobbie, old chap. Two of us can't very well get lost on this mountain. We'll separate enough to keep within hallooing distance, and we'll tie a handkerchief on this tree so we can get back to it again if we want to. We know we're part way down, anyway. That's certain."

"I don't feel so sure," was Bob's answer. "We ought to have turned back when it began to cloud up; but I never dreamed of snow. The family will be having a blue fit about us."

"Cheer up! We'll get down all right, only it may take us a little longer," Van asserted.

They branched into a side path.

The snow swirled about them in blinding sheets, and their footing became heavy and slippery.

Wandering on, they scanned the trees.

Not a mark appeared.

Both boys were chilled now, and their spirits drooped.

The possibility of being lost on the mountain began to definitely form itself in their minds.

"I'm mighty sorry I got you into this scrape, Van," Bob said after a long pause. "I was too cock-sure of myself. That comes of thinking you know it all."

"Pooh! It wasn't your fault, Bob. I'd give a cent, though, to know where we are. Do you suppose we've been making any progress all this time, or just going round in a circle?"

"Search me. I'll bet we've walked miles," groaned Bob. "I've got to rest if we never find the trail."

He spoke wearily.

"You're not going to sit down, Bob," Van retorted sharply. "Brace up. You've got to keep moving."

"But I can't. I'm tired and--and--sleepy."

His voice trailed off into a yawn.

"I don't care." Van wheeled on his friend fiercely and striding up to him shook him violently by the shoulders. "Now pull yourself together!" he commanded. "Where's your nerve? Brace up or I'll rattle the daylights out of you."

"I can't go another step."

"You've got to. Start on ahead. Don't crawl that way--walk! Faster! Faster than that, do you hear? I'm just behind you, and I shall step on your heels if you lag. Keep it up. Go on."

Panting, Bob obeyed.

Suddenly he gave a cry.

"What's the matter?" demanded Van.

"There! There on the tree!" He pointed before him with trembling hand. "Your sweater!"

Van pushed past him.

"Sure as fate! My sweater! Blamed if it isn't."

They both laughed weakly.

"Then we've found the trail!" Bob almost sobbed the words.

"We sure have! And hark, don't you hear voices? It's David, as I'm alive; and your father!"

Aid had indeed come.

"Father!" Bob shouted the word and then laughed again--this time a bit hysterically.

"The rescuing party's right here!" called Mr. Carlton.

He said it lightly, but as he came up and joined them Van saw that his face was drawn and his eyes suspiciously bright.

"David has the sledge just at the foot of the hill," he remarked, appearing not to notice the boy's fatigue. "I guess you'd just as soon ride the rest of the way."

He slipped an arm around Bob.

"It's not much farther, son. Move right along as fast as you can. Hurry, boy. Your mother's pretty worried. Thank goodness we found you in time."

CHAPTER III

SUGARING OFF

The next morning, incredible as it seemed, Bob and Van were none the worse for their mountain trip, and Mr. Carlton, who had worried no little about them, and who was still feeling the effects of his hours of anxiety, remarked somewhat wrathfully:

"You two fellows come to the surface like a pair of corks! Any one would think that being lost on a mountain was an every-day occurrence with you. That is the difference between sixteen and forty-six, I suppose. My poor old nerves rebel at being jolted in such casual fashion."

Bob smiled.

"We're fit as two fighting cocks to-day, Father," he declared. "In fact, this very minute we're going out to help David collect sap. They are going to boil a lot of it down to-day."

"I imagined as much when I saw the smoke rising from the sugar-house chimney. Well, you seem to have your morning's work mapped out. Just don't get lost again, for I have no mind to go scouring the country a second time to find you."

"We'll take good care, Mr. Carlton," Van replied, giving a final tug at his long rubber boots.

"You may not lose yourself, Van," Bob chuckled, "but I am morally certain you'll lose your boots. You will just walk off and leave them in some snow-drift or mud puddle and never miss them. They are big enough for an elephant. Where did you get them, anyway?"

"They're an old pair David lent me; your father said I'd better wear them."

"He's dead right, too. The snow is still deep in spots, and it is thawing everywhere. It is not the boots I'm quarreling with; it's their size. I guess, though, you can get on somehow. We want to cut across the road and make for that hill over to the right. That's where the sugar-house is; it stands in the middle of an orchard of maples which were planted by my grandfather. Of course we have other maple trees scattered about the farm and David taps those, too; but most of our sugar comes from this orchard."

"Did your grandfather make maple-sugar to sell?"

"Goodness, no! He made it to use. White sugar, you must understand, was not so common in the olden days as it is now. Very little of it was grown in our country; and so, as it had to be brought from the East Indies, Spain, and South America, it was pretty expensive. Grandfather told me once that when he was a boy people used brown sugar or maple-sugar to sweeten their food, and sometimes they even used cheap molasses. White sugar was looked upon as a great luxury."

"I don't think I ever realized that before," said Van thoughtfully.

"Why, even my father remembers when, as a little shaver, he used to have white sugar spread on his bread for a treat."

"Seems queer, doesn't it?" Van mused.

"Yes. But it isn't so queer when you consider that all the sugar-cane now growing in America first had to be brought to the West Indies from Spain, the Canary Islands, or Madeira and then transplanted along the Mississippi delta. Dad says that originally sugar-cane came from Africa or India and that doubtless it was the Crusaders who introduced it into Europe."

"Do you mean to tell me that people never knew about sugar until then?" inquired Van incredulously, halting in the middle of the road.

"The Chinese were practically the only people who did, and they did not use it at all as we do; they just sweetened things with the thin sap."

Van regarded his chum steadily for a moment.

"Say," he demanded at last, "how did you come to know so much, Bobbie?"

"What? Oh, about sugar? I don't know much. I just happen to remember a few scraps Father has told me from time to time. He's in the sugar business, you know."

"Really? No, I didn't know. You never said anything about it. Cane-sugar?"

"Yes." Bob watched Van curiously.

"That's odd."

"Why?"

"Oh, because my father is in the sugar business too. Don't you recall my telling your father so? Yes, my dad makes beet sugar."

"Then that's how my father happened to know your father!" exclaimed Bob quickly. "I suppose they're business friends. I've been wondering why Father kept watching you. Probably he sees in you some resemblance to your father. Do you look like him?"

"I hardly know. Some people think I do. My mother says so," was Van's indifferent response. "But say, tell me more about sugar. You'd think with my father right in the business I'd know something about it; but I don't. Do they get sugar from anything beside beets, and sugar-cane, and maple sap?"

"Oh, my, yes. There's sugar in ever so many other things: in grapes, and milk, and the date palm, and in maize; but it is from the beet and cane that the most sugar can be extracted."

Van nodded.

"You're quite a lecturer, Bobbie," he said. "Wait until I get back home and astonish my father with all this knowledge. I'll make his eyes stick out."

Van broke into hearty laughter at the thought. Then, as he started to walk on he gave a shout of dismay.

"Hold onto me, Bob," he cried. "I can't move. While I've been standing here listening to your words of wisdom I've been sinking deeper and deeper into your old yellow mud until now I can't stir. I can't--upon my word. My feet are in perfectly solid. You can laugh if you want to, but you've just got to pull me out, that's all. Help! Help! To the rescue. I shall disappear in another minute. David will never see his rubber boots again."

"Of course you can get your feet out," was Bob's scornful retort.

"Cross my heart I can't. Honest, Bobbie," protested Van. "I've got into a quicksand or a quagmire or something. Look at me. I'm up to my knees now, and if you don't hurry you'll see nothing of me but my collar. I saved your life yesterday; you might do the same for me to-day."

But Bob was too convulsed with amusement to offer aid; instead he stood on a large rock at the roadside and laughed immoderately.

"Pull! Pull!" he cried to Van. "Why don't you pull?"

"I am pulling," Van answered. "But it does no good. I can't budge my feet. I never saw such mud in all my life. It must be yards deep. It sucks my boots right off. You'll have to help me."

"Not I! I know too well what would happen. It would be like Kipling's story of the Elephant's Child. Don't you remember, when the crocodile let go the nose of the little elephant how he suddenly sat down *plop*. I've no notion of being pulled into this mud hole when your rubber boots come to the surface. You'll have to get yourself out."

"You old heathen! It is not a straight game to fit me out with a pair of hip rubber boots miles too large for me and then sit and howl when you see me losing my life in them. Well, you needn't come into the mire if you don't want to, but you can at least be gentleman enough to pass me the end of that pole that is lying beside you," said Van.

"I'll do that."

Bob picked up a long branch from the ground.

"Here!" he cried. "Catch hold of this and pull."

The two boys tugged at opposite ends of the stick.

Then suddenly and quite without warning something happened.

The dead wood parted and Bob hurtled backward off the rock where he had been standing and landed in a snow-drift; while Van, much to his astonishment, sat down with abruptness in the wettest of the mud.

Two more chagrined boys could nowhere have been found.

Bob was the first to get to his feet. Shaking the snow out of his hair and collar he called:

"Get up, you--unless you want to be swallowed up for life. My eye, but you're a sight! If your mother could only see you now. Well, your feet are out, if you did have to get in all over to do it. Now step lively if you don't want to get stuck again. You are a peach, I must say!"

Van took the banter good-naturedly.

"That's what one might call being buried alive," he answered. "Lucky it wasn't you! I'm tall and could keep my head out; but the mire would long since have closed over an abbreviated person like yourself and you would have been seen no more."

Bob winced. He was sensitive about his height.

Clambering up on the rock beside his chum Van scooped up a handful of clean snow and with it washed his hands and face.

"There!" he said at length. "I'm just as tidy as if it had not happened."

"I can't exactly agree with you," replied Bob, "but I guess you'll have to do. Come on now. Goodness only knows where David and the sledge have got to by this time."

They hurried up the hill.

"There's David!" Van said, as they reached the crest of the rise.

It was David sure enough; and standing beside him in his customary motionless attitude was the Admiral harnessed into a great sledge surmounted by a barrel into which David was pouring the sap as fast as he gathered it. At the moment the man was busy detaching one of the sap buckets from the trunk of a giant maple.

The boys joined him.

"What are you doing, Dave?" asked Van curiously.

"Doing! Ain't you got eyes, young man? I certainly ain't writing a book or taking a wireless message," he answered without turning his head.

"But straight, I mean it. What are you doing? You know this business is new to me," explained Van.

"Haven't you ever seen maple-sugar made?" David's tone was full of surprise.

"Never."

"Well, bless my soul! Where was you raised?"

"In Colorado."

"Humph! That accounts for it. If you'd been brought up in the East you'd have known."

"But I was raised in the East, David, and I've never seen maple-sugar made," piped Bob, instantly overthrowing the old farmer's philosophy.

"You ain't never--you ain't seen maple-syrup or maple-sugar made, Mr. Bob?" queried David aghast.

"No."

"Well, what are we coming to?"

The farmhand surveyed the boys disdainfully.

"What you been doing with yourself all your days?" he gasped at last.

"I've been going to school."

"And they ain't taught you to make maple-sugar? That's about all schooling is worth nowadays," he affirmed. "Now I warn't never inside a schoolhouse in my life, but I've known from the time I was knee-high to a grasshopper how to make maple-sugar. I made pounds of it before I was half the age of you two. The boys of this generation don't know nothin'!"

He sniffed contemptuously.

"Well, you may as well learn before you're a minute older," he continued. "Listen, now. Do you see the little hole in this maple?" He pointed up at the gray trunk above his head. "We make a little hole like that in every tree as soon as the sap begins to run in the early spring. Then we drive into the hole this small piece of hollow wood--it is like a trough, you see; and the sap runs through it into the buckets we hang beneath. All day and all night it drips in and each morning we go round and empty every pail into the cask we carry on the sledge. The sap, as you see, is thin, because only part of it is sugar; the rest is water. What we have to do is to boil down the liquid until the part that is water goes off in vapor and only the syrup is left. If we're after maple-syrup we let it cool when it gets thick and later bottle it; but if we want sugar we must boil the syrup still more until little crystals form in it."

"How can you tell when it has been boiled enough?" questioned Van.

"Oh, we've made it enough times to know," David replied. "Some folks stick a thermometer into it and figger how hot it will have to be; they say that's the best way. Others try the syrup in cold water or on snow like you would candy. Generally speaking, I can tell by the feel of it, and by the way it drips from the spoon. Sometimes, though, when I'm in doubt I try it on snow myself. If it gets kinder soft and waxy you can be sure it is getting done. If I was you instead of tracking round emptying buckets I'd go in the sugar-house and see 'em boiling the syrup. They started yesterday, and as I calculate it the mess ought to be pretty well along by now."

"Bully idea, David! What do you say, Van?" asked Bob. "Shall we trail David or shall we go in and see the sugar made?"

"Sugar! Sugar! Me for the sugar!" Van cried.

"Sugar it is then!"

Into the sugar-house they went.

The small room was hot and steamy, and in the middle of it in a zinc-lined tank the foaming sap was boiling furiously. Beside it stood McMasters, Mr. Carlton's foreman, a thermometer in his hand.

"Good-morning, Mr. Bob," he said. "So you are coming to cast an eye on the maple-sugar! Last week we made syrup and bottled it. Not a bad day's work, eh?"

With no little pride he pointed to a row of neat bottles symmetrically arranged on a shelf. "We'll seal them to-morrow or next day and get the labels on, and then they will be ready to sell. But to-day it's sugar, so we have to keep the sap at a higher temperature."

As he spoke he paused to test the bubbling liquid in the kettle.

"If you lads want a treat take one of those wooden plates over there and fill it with snow; I'll spoon some of this hot sap over it, and you will have a feast for a king."

The boys needed no urging. They took the plates, hurried out, and soon returned with them; over the heap of snow the foreman poured several heaping spoonfuls of hot syrup which, to their surprise, cooled in an incredibly short time and stiffened into a sticky mass that looked like candy.

"Now get one of those wooden skewers from the shelf and use it as a fork," McMasters said.

The boys caught the idea at once.

They gathered the candied syrup up on the end of the sticks and thrust it into their mouths.

"Why, it is just like toffy!" Van exclaimed.

"It is a sight fresher than anything you could buy at the store," observed the foreman.

"I believe I've got to have some more, Mac," Bob said. "Somehow it melts away before you know you're eating it."

He refilled his plate with fresh snow and held it out for a second helping of syrup.

McMasters filled it good-naturedly.

But when the plates were extended the fourth and fifth time the Scotchman demurred.

"It is no stuff to make a meal of, Mr. Bob," protested he. 'And at ten o'clock in the morning, too. I'll give you no more. It is too sweet. Next you know the two of you will be spending your vacation in bed and wondering what's the matter with you. Why, we'd have no sugar at all if you should stay here eating at this rate. If it's candy you're wantin', ask the cook to boil some maple-syrup until it is thick like molasses candy; then turn it out of the pan and when it is almost cool pull it until it turns white. You'll find it better than any candy you can buy. Try it."

"We certainly will, Mac, and thanks for the suggestion," Bob replied.

"And while you're at it you might hunt up some butternuts and stir them in; I'll recommend the result and will wager you'll think it as good as anything you ever ate."

Once more he took the temperature of the steaming sap.

"We're going to put some of the sugar in those tin pails and sell it," he continued. "Each pail holds ten pounds. And some we shall pour into those small tin moulds and make little scalloped cakes for our own use. I reckon you can have some of them to take back to college when you go. We'll certainly have a plenty to spare you some, for your father will make a handsome thing out of his sugar this year. I wouldn't wonder but you're being educated on maple-sugar money. You better make your bow of thanks to the trees as you go through the orchard," he added whimsically.

CHAPTER IV

THE REFINERY

Vacation with its country sports came to an end only too quickly, and leaving the New Hampshire hills behind the Carlton family, together with Van Blake, set out for New York where the boys were to make a weekend visit before returning to Colversham.

"I wish while we're in New York we could go through your refinery, Dad," Bob remarked to his father.

Mr. Carlton glanced at him in surprise.

"What set you thinking of that, Bob?" he asked. "You never were interested in sugar making before."

"I know it, Father." Bob flushed guiltily. "I ought to have been. But since we have seen maple-sugar made Van and I thought it would be fun to see the process that white sugar has to go through before it is ready for the market."

"Van thought so, did he?" queried Mr. Carlton.

"Why, yes, he thought so. I believe, though, it was I who suggested it."

"Humph!" murmured Mr. Carlton. He mused a moment. "I suppose it would do no harm," he said at last, half to himself.

"Harm!"

"No, no! Of course not," interrupted Mr. Carlton hurriedly. "The process is an open secret anyway, except perhaps--Oh, I guess it would be all right."

Bob regarded his father with a puzzled stare.

"I will arrange for you and Van to go through the works right away," continued Mr. Carlton. "It simply will be necessary for me to telephone the superintendent and tell him you are coming so he will have some one on hand to explain things to you. This was your scheme, you say?"

"Yes, sir. Why?"

"Nothing, nothing," was Mr. Carlton's enigmatic reply.

He was as good as his word, for despite his peculiar reluctance in the matter he lost no time in perfecting the plan, and the next morning after the party reached New York he informed the boys that the motor-car would be at the door at nine o'clock to take them to the refinery.

Bob and Van, to whom New York was more or less of an old story, hailed this announcement with pleasure and promptly stowed themselves away in the big limousine which was to whirl them to Long Island where the works were located. All the way out Van was singularly silent, and appeared to be turning something over in his mind; once he started to speak, but checked himself abruptly.

Bob watched him uneasily.

"I believe you've lost your enthusiasm about sugar," said he at last, "and did not really want to come."

"What a notion! Of course I wanted to come."

"But you seem so glum, old man."

"Glum! Nonsense! I never was in better spirits in my life."

With a sudden shifting of the subject Van pointed to a stack of chimneys cleaving the sky and observed:

"I wonder if those belong to your father's plant?"

"I fancy they do," was Bob's quick answer. "Dad said we'd see a bunch of tall chimneys, and that the refinery was of yellow brick."

"Then this is the place," Van declared, drumming on the window glass with forced gaiety.

He did not, however, leap from the car with the spring of anticipation that Bob did, and noticing his spiritless step his friend once more remarked upon it.

"You seem bored to death to have to drag yourself through here, Van," said he. "What's the matter? You know if you do not want to come you don't have to."

"I do want to."

"But somehow you seem so-so--"

"So _what?_"

"Why, you seem to hang back as if you could hardly put one foot before the other," answered Bob. "Don't you feel well?"

"Prime! There's nothing the matter with me. What put that idea into your head?"

"Chiefly you yourself."

"Well, cut it out. I don't see what you're fussing about me for. I'm just as anxious to see how sugar is made as you are."

Still Bob was unconvinced. He could not have explained why, but he felt certain that Van's enthusiasm was feigned. For a second he paused undecidedly on the pavement before the door of the great factory; then shrugging his shoulders he entered, followed closely by his chum.

It was evident that they were expected, for a clerk rose from his desk and came forward to greet them.

"Mr. Hennessey, the superintendent, said I was to bring you to his office when you arrived," he said.

"Thank you."

"You are Mr. Carlton's son, aren't you?"

"Yes."

"I thought you must be. Mr. Hennessey himself is going to take you through the works."

The clerk led the way to the door of a private office, where he knocked.

"Mr. Carlton and his friend are here," he announced to the boy who opened the door. "Tell Mr. Hennessey right away."

The boys had not a moment to wait before a large man with a genial face and outstretched hand came forward.

"I'm glad to see you, Mr. Carlton," he said. "I'm Hennessey, the superintendent. Possibly you may have heard your father speak of me; I have been helping him make sugar for twenty years."

Bob smiled up into the eyes of the big man looking down at him.

"Indeed Dad has spoken of you, Mr. Hennessey," he said, returning the hearty hand-shake. "He depends on you a lot. He says he always feels sure that when you're on the job everything will be all right."

Mr. Hennessey flushed with pleasure.

"I merely try to run your father's place as if it were my own," was the modest rejoinder.

"That's just it--that's why Father feels he can go to the North Pole if he wants to and not worry while he's gone," nodded Bob. "I think it is mighty good of you to bother with my chum and me. Can't you send some one to take us through the refinery? There is not the slightest need for you to go with us yourself."

"Oh, I wouldn't think of turning you over to some one else. You see I am interested in your sugar education; I can't allow the boss's son to get a wrong start in the business," laughed Mr. Hennessey.

"I'm afraid I'm not starting in the business," protested Bob, shaking his head deprecatingly. "I'm only trying to learn a little something about Dad's job, so I can be a bit more intelligent about it."

"You're going to investigate the way your father earns his money, eh?" chuckled the superintendent. "Well, I'll tell you right now you need do no blushing for your father's business methods; he makes his fortune as cleanly and honestly as any man could make it."

"I'll take a chance on Dad," was the laconic response.

"You can do so with safety."

There was a pause and turning Bob introduced Van Blake.

Then after the two boys had been provided with duck coats so that none of the sticky liquid that sometimes dripped from the machinery should spot their clothing the three set out for the basement of the factory, where the incoming cargoes of sugar were unloaded. Here great bags or casks of raw sugar were being opened, and their contents emptied into wooden troughs preparatory to cleansing and refining.

Both lads regarded with surprise the material that was being tipped out into the bins.

"Why, it looks like nothing but coarse, muddy snow!" ejaculated Van. "Do you really mean to tell us that you can make that brown stuff white, Mr. Hennessey?"

"That's what we're here for," answered Mr. Hennessey, obviously enjoying his amazement. "All raw sugar comes to us this way. You see, it is about the color of maple or brown sugar, but it is not nearly so pure, for it has a great deal of dirt mixed with it when we first get it."

"Where does it come from?" inquired Bob.

"Largely from the plantations of Cuba and Porto Rico. Toward the end of the year we also get raw sugar from Java, and by the time this is refined and ready for the market the new crop from the West Indies comes along. In addition to this we get consignments from the Philippine Islands, the Hawaiian Islands, South America, Formosa, and Egypt. I suppose it is quite unnecessary to tell you young men anything of how the cane is grown; of course you know all that."

"I don't believe we do, except in a general way," Bob admitted honestly. "I am ashamed to be so green about a thing at which Dad has been working for years. I don't know why I never asked about it before. I guess I never was interested. I simply took it for granted."

"That's the way with most of us," was the superintendent's kindly answer. "We accept many things in the world without actually knowing much about them, and it is not until something brings our ignorance before us that we take the pains to focus our attention and learn about them. So do not be ashamed that you do not know about sugar raising; I didn't when I was your age. Suppose, then, I give you a little idea of what happens before this raw sugar can come to us."

"I wish you would," exclaimed both boys in a breath.

"Probably in your school geographies you have seen pictures of sugar-cane and know that it is a tall perennial not unlike our Indian corn in appearance; it has broad, flat leaves that sometimes measure as many as three feet in length, and often the stalk itself is twenty feet high. This stalk is jointed like a bamboo pole, the joints being about three inches apart near the roots and increasing in distance the higher one gets from the ground."

"How do they plant it?" Bob asked.

"It can be planted from seed, but this method takes much time and patience; the usual way is to plant it from cuttings, or slips. The first growth from these cuttings is called plant cane; after these are taken off the roots send out ratoons or shoots from which the crop of one or two years, and sometimes longer, is taken. If the soil is not rich and moist replanting is more frequently necessary and in places like Louisiana, where there is annual frost, planting must be done each year. When the cane is ripe it is cut and brought from the field to a central sugar mill, where heavy iron rollers crush from it all the juice. This liquid drips through into troughs from which it is carried to evaporators where the water portion of the sap is eliminated and the juice left; you would be surprised if you were to see this liquid. It looks like nothing so much as the soapy, bluish-gray dish-water that is left in the pan after the dishes have been washed."

"A tempting picture!" Van exclaimed.

"I know it. Sugar isn't very attractive during its process of preparation," agreed Mr. Hennessey. "The sweet liquid left after the water has been extracted is then poured into vacuum pans to be boiled until the crystals form in it, after which it is put into whirling machines, called centrifugal machines, that separate the dry sugar from the syrup with which it is mixed. This syrup is later boiled into molasses. The sugar is then dried and packed in these burlap sacks such as you see here, or in hogsheads, and shipped to refineries to be cleansed and whitened."

"Isn't any of the sugar refined in the places where it grows?" queried Bob.

"Practically none. Large refining plants are too expensive to be erected everywhere; it therefore seems better that they should be built in our large cities, where the shipping facilities are good not only for receiving sugar in its raw state but for distributing it after it has been refined and is ready for sale. Here, too, machinery can more easily be bought and the business handled with less difficulty."

"You spoke of a central sugar mill," began Bob.

"Yes. Each plantation does not have a mill of its own or, indeed, need one. Frequently a planter will raise too small a crop to pay him to operate a mill; so a mill is constructed in the center of a sugar district, and to this growers may carry their wares and be paid in bulk. It saves much trouble and expense. It also encourages small growers who could not afford to build mills and might in consequence abandon sugar raising. The leaves are all stripped off before the cane is shipped so that nothing but the stalks are sent. As the largest portion of sugar is in the part of the cane nearest the ground it is cut as close to the root as possible. After the juice has been crushed from the stalks by putting them several times through the rollers the cane, or *begass*, as it is called, is so dry that it can be used as fuel for running the mill machinery."

"How clever!"

"Clever and economical as well," agreed Mr. Hennessey. "Moreover, it does away with a waste product that otherwise would accumulate."

Bob nodded.

"Raw sugar has usually been shipped to the northern refineries by water, as that mode of transportation is cheaper; but during the Great War ships have been so scarce that in 1916 a large consignment of Hawaiian sugar was for the first time sent overland across the American continent by train; this of course made the freight rates higher, and if such a condition were to continue the price of sugar would of necessity have to be advanced."

"I never thought of such things affecting us," murmured Van.

"We live in a network of interdependence," Mr. Hennessey replied. "Scarcely anything can be done in any land that does not affect us. Commercial conditions react upon us all, for there is not one of us who is not indebted to the four corners of the globe for what he eats, wears, and uses. Therefore, you see, world prosperity and comfort can be at their height only when there is world peace under which all nations are friends, maintaining cordial trade relation with one another."

"What political party do you belong to, Mr. Hennessey?" asked Bob, glancing into the superintendent's earnest face.

"I do not know just what label you would put on me," the big man replied evasively. "But this I do know: first, last, and all the time I am for a universe where each country shall work for the good of the whole."

He spoke slowly and with impressiveness; then breaking off abruptly he led the way up a winding iron staircase and the boys, still pondering his words, followed him silently and thoughtfully.

CHAPTER V

VAN SPRINGS A SURPRISE

The room into which they emerged was at the top of the factory, and it was here in great vats that the dry sugar was melted.

"We often melt down as many as two million pounds of raw sugar a day," said Mr. Hennessey. "The United States, you know, is the greatest sugar consuming nation in the world. No other country devours so much of it. One reason is because here even the poorer classes have money enough so they can afford sugar for household use; in many countries this is not the case. Only the well-to-do take sugar in tea or coffee and have it for common use. Our Americans also eat quantities of candy. At the present time children eat three times as many sweets as did their parents, and the amount is constantly increasing. Doctors tell us sugar is one of the fuels necessary to the human system; it generates both heat and energy. Possibly it is because our people work so hard and are driven at such high nervous tension that they demand so much of this sort of food."

"I never knew before that candy was good for us," ejaculated Bob in surprise.

"Oh, bless you, yes! But you must take it in moderation if you wish to benefit from it and escape illness. Used intelligently sugar is an excellent food, but of course you must prescribe it for yourself in the proper proportions," laughed Mr. Hennessey. "We all constantly take more or less sugar into our systems through the ordinary foods we eat. But here in America over and above this each individual annually averages about eighty pounds of sugar. You will agree that that is a good deal."

"I should think so! Why, that is a tremendous amount!" Van declared.

"It seems so when you see it in figures, doesn't it?" returned the superintendent. "Next to the United States in sugar consumption comes England, the reason for this being that the English manufacture such vast amounts of jam for the market. England is a great fruit growing country, you must remember. The damp, moderate climate results in wonderful strawberries, gooseberries, plums, and other small fruits. With these products cheap, fine, and plenty, the English have taken up fruit canning as one of their industries, and they turn out some of the best jams and marmalades that are made."

The boys listened intently.

"The Germans and the French are much more frugal than we Americans," went on Mr. Hennessey. "Sugar is not so common in their countries. Often when in Germany you will notice people in the restaurants and cafés who carry away in their pockets the loaf sugar which has been allotted them and which they have not had occasion to use. It is a common occurrence, and considered quite proper, although it looks strange to us. Doubtless, too, if you have traveled abroad you have discovered how few candy shops there are. Foreigners regard the wholesale fashion in which we devour sweets with wonder and often with disgust. They consider it a form of self-indulgence, and indeed I myself think we are at times a bit immoderate."

"My father says we are an immoderate people," Van put in.

"I am afraid he is right," nodded Mr. Hennessey. "We seem to proceed on the principle that if a thing is good we must have a great deal of it. However, the vice--if vice it be--is good for the sugar business."

He paused a moment and stood looking down into the great foaming vats before him.

"You can't see the steam coils that are melting this raw sugar," he remarked. "They go round the inside of the tanks. But after the liquid is drawn off you can see them. When first melted the sugar is far from pure; you would be astonished at the amount of dirt mixed with it. Many of these impurities boil up to the surface and over and over again we skim them off. But even after that we have to wash the sugar by various processes. After it has been separated, clarified, and filtered it comes out a clear white liquid, and is ready for the vacuum pans, where the water is evaporated and the sugar crystallized."

"How do you get the liquid clear?" asked Bob.

"After it has been skimmed as carefully as possible we first settle it through the agency of chemicals," answered Mr. Hennessey. "We use milk of lime as a foundation, but we put other things with it. Our exact formula is a secret, but since you are in the family I guess there would be no objection to my telling you that we use---"

"Don't tell us! Don't tell us!" cried Van suddenly. "I don't want to know. I'd rather not. I mustn't listen."

Covering his ears the boy turned away.

His companions regarded him with amazement.

"Don't tell me, Mr. Hennessey," he pleaded. "Don't tell me anything that is secret. I can't listen. It wouldn't be right."

It was evident both to the superintendent and to Bob that his distress was real, and although neither of them understood it Mr. Hennessey cut short his explanation.

Try as they would the strange interruption left a jarring note behind it, and to ease the tenseness the older man stepped forward and, taking from a rack near by one of several glass tubes filled with yellow liquid, held it up to the light.

"You see much must still be done to this stuff before it comes out white," he said. "We squeeze the liquid through a series of filter bags and also send it through other filters filled with black bone coal."

"What is black bone coal?" Bob demanded.

"Bone coal is a product made by burning and pulverizing the large bones left at the abbatoirs until a coarse-grained black powder not unlike emery sand is made; if this is not allowed to become too fine with using it is an excellent sugar filter. In fact, strangely enough, nothing has ever been found to take its place, and it has become a necessary but expensive agency employed in every sugar refinery. Quantities of it are used; in our refinery alone we have about a hundred bone coal filters and each one holds thirty tons of black bone coal. That will give you some idea how much of it is needed. We get nothing back on it, either, for in the process of using it becomes finer, and after that it is good for nothing unless, perhaps, to be made into cheap shoe-dressing. Unlike many of the other industries sugar refining has no by-products; by that I mean nothing on which the manufacturer may recover money. On the contrary in the leather business, for example, almost every scrap of material can either be utilized or sold for cash; odds and ends of the hides go into glue stock, small bits of leather are made into heel-taps or hardware fittings. But in refining cane-sugar there is nothing to be turned back into money to reimburse the manufacturer for his outlay. What isn't sugar is dead loss."

The three now moved on and saw how the heated juice traveled by means of pipes from one vat to another, and how it constantly became thicker and clearer.

"One of the greatest dangers to successful sugar making is fermentation," observed Mr. Hennessey. "Sugar must continually be stirred by revolving paddles to keep it from fermenting; we also are obliged to take the greatest care that our vats and all other receptacles are clean, and that the plant is immaculate. Frequently we wash down all the walls with a solution of lime in order that the entire interior of the refinery may be quite fresh."

"I didn't dream it was so much work to make white sugar," ventured Bob, a little awed. "Our maple-sugar making was much simpler."

"I'll venture to say it was," agreed Mr. Hennessey. "In the first place, you did not make such a quantity of it; then you did not try to get it white. Furthermore, you were content to take it in cakes. Making cane-sugar is, however, easy enough if one is careful and knows the exact way to do it. There is plenty of opportunity to spoil it--I'll admit that; but it is seldom that a batch of our sugar goes back on us. We have fine chemists who watch every step of the process and who constantly test samples of the liquid at every stage into which it passes until it comes out water-white."

"And then?"

"Then follows crystallization, and this too requires skilled workmen and extreme care. The water is evaporated and the sugar crystallized in the vacuum pans, the size crystal depending upon the temperature at which the liquid is boiled. It takes a lower temperature to form a small crystal and a higher one to form a large crystal. An expert who takes the temperature of the boiling sugar regulates what we call fine-grain or coarse-grain sugar by regulating the size of the crystals. By drawing off some of the liquid and examining it on a glass slide by electric light he can tell the precise moment at which the crystals are the right size. Each size has a name by which it is known in the trade: Diamond A; Fine Granulated; Coarse Granulated; Crystal Domino; Confectioners' A and so on."

They were walking as Mr. Hennessey talked. "After the sugar has been crystallized in the pans it passes into a mixer, where it is stirred and kept from caking until it is put into the centrifugal machines, which actually spin off the crystals. These machines are lined with gauze, and as they whirl at tremendous velocity they force out through this gauze the liquid part of the sugar and leave the sugar crystals inside the machine. When these are quite dry the bottom of the receptacle opens, and the granular sugar is dropped through into a large bin."

"But I should think it would stick together," objected Van.

"That's an intelligent objection, my boy," declared Mr. Hennessey, much pleased at Van's grasp of the subject. "It would stick if it were not dried off by a degree of heat just right to keep the particles separate and not allow them to cake. After this any dust or dirt adhering to the sugar is blown off by an air blast. The product is then ready to be pressed into moulds or cut; boxed in small packages of varying weights; or put into bags or barrels."

Mr. Hennessey led the way to another floor of the refinery.

[Illustration: "I SHOULD THINK IT WOULD STICK TOGETHER."]

Here were automatic machines upon which empty boxes traveled along until they reached a device that filled each one with the exact number of pounds to be contained in it, the package afterward passed to women who sealed it tightly and gave it the final touch before it was shipped. Other women were packing loaf or domino sugar, while down-stairs in a cooper shop men moved about constructing with great rapidity the barrels that were to carry larger quantities of sugar to the wholesale and retail stores.

"I guess by this time you've had all the sugar-making you want for one day," declared the superintendent. "I'm afraid I've given you quite a stiff lesson. You see I am so interested in it myself that I forget to have mercy on my listeners."

He smiled down at the boys.

"I'm sure we have had a fine morning with you, Mr. Hennessey, and we certainly have learned a lot," Bob said, putting out his hand. "I can't swear, though, that we could make white sugar even now."

"Faith, I'd be sorry if I thought I could teach any one the whole process in three hours. It would make my twenty years of study and hard work brand me as pretty stupid," chuckled the big superintendent.

CHAPTER VI

A FAMILY TANGLE

It was not until the boys were in the motor-car and returning home that Bob ventured to mention to Van his strange behavior of the morning.

"What on earth was the matter with you, Van?" he asked.

Van stirred uneasily.

"Bobbie," he said, "I'm going to tell you something. I've been wondering whether I'd better or not, and at last I've decided to. I didn't want to go to your father's refinery to-day or, in fact, at all. You've all been very kind to me, although it was not until I got a letter from my father this morning that I realized how kind."

He paused.

"Has your dad told you anything about my people?" he asked abruptly. "Of course he knows, but he may have thought best to keep it to himself; at any rate it has not prevented him from giving me as cordial a welcome to your home as he would if--"

"If what?"

"Well, if I weren't the person I am."

"What do you mean?"

"Why, he's trusted me and treated me as if he really liked me; and yet under the circumstances you can't expect him actually to mean it."

"Mean what? What are you talking about?"

"Hasn't he spoken to you about my father?"

"Of course not; why should he?"

"Then you haven't heard anything?"

"Not a word. I don't understand what you are driving at at all," Bob declared, somewhat irritated. "Out with it. What's the matter?"

Van hesitated as if uncertain how to begin.

"That's mighty white of your father," he murmured, breaking the pause. "You see, it is this way. When I wrote home that I was going to New Hampshire to visit my roommate the family wrote me to go ahead. I recall now that I didn't mention your last name; in fact I guess I haven't in any of my letters. When I did happen to write (which wasn't often) I've always spoken of you as *Bob*. So when I got to Allenville I dropped a line to Father to say I'd arrived safely and in the note I put something about Mr. Carlton. Father lit on it right away; he wished to know who these Carltons were. I replied they were Mr. and Mrs. Carlton, of course--the parents of my roommate. Upon that I got another letter from home in which Father inquired if your father was in the sugar business, and said that years ago he used to have a partner named James Carlton, who started in the sugar trade with him and with whom he later quarreled. He supposed this could not be the same person, but he just wondered if by any chance it was."

Van stopped.

"Was that all he said?"

"No, but I don't like to tell you the rest, Bobbie."

"Fire away--unless it is something about Dad," Bob replied. "If it is I shan't listen, or at least I shan't believe it."

"It isn't exactly against your father. I do not understand it very well myself. My father just said that if your father was Mr. James Carlton and he was in the sugar business he felt that because of family misunderstandings it would be better if I did not visit here again. He was very sorry I had done it this time, but of course that could not be helped now."

"You don't mean to say he wants you to break off your friendship with me?" Bob gasped tremulously.

"No, he didn't seem to be opposed to you; he just was hot at your dad. He added that he didn't believe your family could have known who I was when they asked me here, and I am afraid that's true, Bobbie."

"Why, of course they knew! Haven't I spoken of you over and over again?" Bob protested indignantly.

Van shook his head.

"They knew I was your chum all right, Bob; but so far as details were concerned your family did not know much more about me than mine knew about you. Don't you recall how, when I arrived at Allenville, your father asked if I was one of the _Sugar Blakes_ --Asa Blake's son?"

"Yes, I do remember that now, but--"

"That, you will recollect, was after I was landed at Allenville and your guest. Your father didn't know until that moment who I was, and when he found out he was too decent to say anything, or make it evident he didn't want me in the house. What could he do?"

"But--but--"

Bob broke off from sheer inability to continue. He was much too bewildered.

"Your father sensed the awkwardness of the situation at once. Here you had gone to school and as ill luck would have it you had picked from out the entire bunch of boys the son of his worst enemy for a chum. Neither your father nor mine realized the truth until you innocently carted me home with you for a holiday visit. When your father found out the fact he was too polite to turn me out-of-doors; he just acted the gentleman and made the best of a bad dilemma," explained Van with appalling convincingness. "He even had the goodness to save my life the day we got lost on one of your New Hampshire mountains. He didn't tell you any of this because he didn't want to spoil your pleasure; but I am certain that if he had known who I was before I came he would not have allowed you to ask me into your home."

"Nonsense! You are way off. Why, he's been as interested in having you with us as I have; at least he has acted so."

"*Acted* is just the word," Van cut in. "He has acted, all right. I guess you'll find he's been acting all the time. Honor bright, hasn't he said anything to you about me?"

"No, not one word." Then suddenly Bob flushed; the memory of his father's strange conversation about the boy's visit to the refinery rushed over him. "Dad did say one thing which I did not understand at the time," he confessed reluctantly. "Perhaps, though, he did not mean anything by it."

"What was it?"

Bob struggled to evade the issue.

"Oh, it was nothing much."

"Come, Bobbie, you and I are friends," interrupted Van, "and we want to keep on being friends no matter how our fathers feel toward one another. If they have quarreled it is a great pity, but at least we needn't. The only way to straighten out this tangle is to be honest with each other and get at the truth; then, and not until then shall we know where we stand."

"You're a brick, Van!"

"Come ahead then--let's have it. What was it your father said?"

"He merely asked whether it was your plan or mine to visit the refinery, and when I told him I suggested it he inquired all over again if I was sure you did not mention it first," Bob returned in very low tone. The words seemed wrung from him, and he colored as he repeated them.

"Was that all?"

"Not quite. After I had convinced him that the trip was my own idea he said: '_Well, well--it can do no harm; the process is an open secret, anyway._'"

"You see I was right in my guess as to his feelings, Bobbie."

"Maybe."

"Of course I was; this proves it."

"I'm afraid so," whispered Bob miserably.

"Now all this may explain to you why I was so queer when we were at the refinery this morning," Van continued, once more reverting to the subject. "Do you understand it any better?"

"I can see you didn't want Mr. Hennessey to tell you much about his processes."

"You bet I didn't. I was in an awful hole. I got that letter from my father just before we left the house, and I was all upset over it. I didn't know what to do. It was bad enough to be visiting you without being shown all through your father's business plant as if I were an honored guest. It didn't seem as if I ought to go at all. If your father knew who I was he certainly couldn't want me to; and if he didn't it was worse yet. At first I thought the only honorable thing was to go straight to him and have it out; but I found I hadn't the nerve. Then I thought I'd ride with you to the factory and not go in. What I dreaded was that we might run into something that I should have no right to see, and that was precisely what happened."

"So that was the reason you stopped Mr. Hennessey when he started to tell us the chemical formula?"

"Yes. He said it was a secret, and it seemed to me it would be wrong for me to listen. If I didn't know what that formula was I certainly couldn't tell it, and ignorance might help me out of an awkward position if any one should try to persuade me to."

"You are a trump, old man."

"It was only the square thing toward your father; he has been straight with me and I want to show him that I can be a gentleman, too."

The boys were silent for an interval; then Bob said:

"Now about this snarl, Van--what are we going to do? Certainly we fellows are not going to let this feud of our fathers affect us."

"Not by a jugful!" retorted Van with spirit. "The thing for us to do is to go right on being friends as if nothing had happened. It will make it all the easier that your father knows just who I am, and my father knows exactly who you are; it is franker and more in the open to have it so. If worse comes to worse we can talk the whole thing out with our families, and tell them how we feel. I am sure both your father and mine are too big to spoil a friendship like ours because of some fuss they had years and years ago. No, sir! I'm going to hold on to you, Bobbie, and," he added shyly, "I'm going to hold on to your father, too, if he'll let me, for I like him."

"I'm glad you like Dad," Bob said, flushing with pleasure. "I do myself."

"My dad isn't so bad, either," Van ventured with a dry little smile. "Some time you shall see for yourself."

"I hope so."

"Then it is agreed that we'll stick together, no matter what happens," said Van solemnly.

"Sure thing!"

"Promise."

"You may bank on me," was Bob's earnest answer.

CHAPTER VII

MR. CARLTON MAKES A WAGER AND WINS

As the boys sat at dinner that evening Mr. Carlton inquired about their trip to the refinery, and with a humorous twinkle in his eye added:

"I do not suppose you would care to put in another day on factory visiting, would you?"

"What do you mean, Dad?" asked Bob.

"I was wondering whether you would like to see where some of our sugar goes," was his father's answer. "Would you be interested to take a tour through the Eureka Candy Factory to-morrow and learn how candy is made?"

"I should," responded Bob promptly.

"And you, Van?" demanded Mr. Carlton with a kindly smile.

"I'd like it of all things," said Van, returning the smile frankly.

"Very well. You shall spend to-morrow at the Eureka Company's factory. They are big customers of ours and when I telephoned them today they told me they would be glad to have you come, and promised to show you all about."

"Are you sure they would want me to come, Mr. Carlton?" asked Van, looking squarely into the eyes of the older man.

"Why not? You're a chum of Bob's, aren't you?"

"Yes. But, you see, that isn't all."

With one searching glance Mr. Carlton scanned the lad's face.

"No, Van," he replied with quiet emphasis, "that is not all. You are more than Bob's chum--you are a friend of mine, too."

The boy flushed.

"I'd like to think so, Mr. Carlton."

"I want you to know so, Van. I happened to see Mr. Hennessey," he went on in a lower tone, "and he related to me that incident at the factory. Of course he did not understand it, but I did--instantly. I appreciated your sense of honor, my boy."

"I wanted to be square."

"You were a gentleman in the very best sense of the word."

A great gladness glowed in Van's eyes, for terse as was the phrase it bore to him the very recognition he had coveted from Bob's father. Mr. Carlton, however, did not enlarge upon the subject, but casting it swiftly into the background asked:

"Are you sure you both would rather spend your last morning in New York going through a candy factory than doing anything else? Factories are tiresome places, you must remember."

"But a candy factory could never be tiresome!" asserted Bob

His father laughed.

"There are just as many miles in a candy factory as any other," he replied. "Any of the men who work there would tell you that, I fancy."

"But they are such nice miles!" argued Bob. "Don't you say we go, Van?"

"I sure do. I want to see how they dip chocolates," Van answered.

"It's all aboard to-morrow morning, then," Mr. Carlton said as he lit his after-dinner cigar.

"There's one thing, Dad, that it's only fair to warn you about," called Bob, turning on the lowest step of the stairway to address his father. "Our expedition may cost you something. You see they probably won't let us eat any candy at the factory; we'll just have to walk round with our eyes open and our hands crammed into our pockets to keep from swiping it. All the time we'll be getting up a tremendous candy appetite, and the minute we get outside we'll just have to make a bee-line for the first candy shop in sight and get filled up. So you must be prepared to cash in for refreshments."

The corners of Mr. Carlton's mouth twisted into an enigmatic smile.

"I'll agree to pay for as much candy as you care to eat," he said, accepting the challenge without objection.

Bob stared at him.

"Do you mean it?"

"Certainly. Why do you question it?"

"But"--faltered Bob in amazement, "you never promised anything like that before."

"I may never promise it again, so make the most of it," was the dry retort.

Although Bob did not reply he by no means forgot the unprecedented offer, and that the memory of it might be equally fresh in his father's mind he spoke of it once again when the three parted the next morning.

"Well, Dad, we're off for the Bonbon World," he called as he passed the library door where his father sat looking over the morning's mail. "Remember you are going to O.K. any candy bills we run up."

"I'm backing you for all you can eat," nodded Mr. Carlton.

"Dad sure is game!" Bob declared as he and Van stepped into the waiting motor-car and began their ride to the factory. "He'll play it out, too. He never goes back on his word."

"I'm afraid he'll be in for something then," grinned Van.

Both boys were more than ever convinced of the truth of this remark when they entered the factory and were greeted by the mingled aroma of chocolate, wintergreen and molasses.

"I could eat ten pounds of chocolates this minute!" exclaimed Van.

"Go easy. Remember, we've got to wait until we have made the entire tour of this factory before we can have so much as a single caramel. You mustn't go getting up your appetite so soon."

"But smell it, Bobbie! Why, the whole place is one mellifluous smudge. What do you say we chuck Colversham and get a job here? Think of having pounds of candy--tons of it--around all the time! Wouldn't it be a snap!"

Van was cut short in his rhapsody by the approach of a pleasant faced lad of about his own age who was dressed from head to foot in white and wore a little white cap, across the front of which was printed in gold letters the word *Eureka*.

"Are you Mr. Carlton?" he inquired of Van.

"I'm not, but my chum is."

"We were expecting you," the boy answered, turning to Bob. "I am to show you and your friend through the works. Will you kindly step this way?"

Tagging at the heels of their white-robed guide Bob and Van made their way through a large storeroom stacked to the ceiling with fancy boxes of various sizes, shapes, and colors.

"Give up Colversham, Bob, and maybe you could come here and wear a white suit every day and personally conduct visitors through the works; perhaps they'd even pay you in bonbons," whispered Van.

"He must be about our age," returned Bob. "I wonder what they pay him."

"I'd lots rather have had a man take us round," said Van softly. "Do you suppose this fellow knows anything?"

All the way up in the elevator the two visitors watched the white-suited boy curiously and when they alighted in the large, sun-flooded room at the top of the factory they were still speculating as to his age and how much he earned, and marveling that so young a representative should have been selected to explain to them the candy industry.

The room they entered was high and airy and at the further end of it, moving amid steam that rose from a score of copper kettles, a great many men in spotless white were hurrying about.

"It is here that we start our candy making," said the boy who was showing Bob about. "Into those copper kettles we put our mixture of confectioners' sugar--confectioners' A, we call it--and corn syrup; this combination forms the basis of almost every variety of candy made. The kettles, as you will see, are heated by gas, which gives a steady flame, and at the side of each one we have a thermometer by which we can tell the exact temperature of the mixture. There is also a glass disc set in the side of every kettle to enable us to watch the boiling. The sugar and corn syrup are melted together and cooked at the temperature which after repeated experiments has proved the most successful for our purpose--one that will neither burn nor stick, or make the cooled fondant too thin to keep its shape."

The boy spoke in the slow, measured tones of one who had told the tale many times before and was quite accustomed to his task.

Bob glanced at Van.

Their respect for the lad was rising.

"How much does one of these kettles hold?" Bob asked.

"About six hundred pounds."

"And you fill all of them every day?" demanded Van in astonishment.

"Several times over," was the answer. "It takes a lot of this ground material for the different kinds; some of it has other ingredients mixed with it later, and some is beaten, flavored, and colored for the fillings of chocolates."

"But who on earth eats so much candy?" ejaculated Bob.

"I don't know," responded the boy wearily. "I'm sure I don't."

"What?"

"I don't believe I'd touch a piece of candy for a hundred dollars," he continued. "I am sick of the sight of it. Candy from morning to night--candy, candy, candy! Candy everywhere! Nothing but candy."

Bob and Van eyed him unbelievingly.

Could a boy be human and feel that way?

"Everybody here gets into the same state of mind," the lad went on. "When the green hands come they are crazy about the stuff for about a couple of days; then it is all over. You couldn't hire them to eat. Every few weeks the different employees are allowed to buy two pounds for themselves at the wholesale price, but you would be surprised to see how few of them do it. If they get it you can be pretty certain that it is to give away, for they'd never eat it themselves."

His two listeners stared incredulously.

Their guide led them across the room.

"So," said he, reverting once more to the kettles and the thermometer, "our candy is not made by guesswork, you see. Sugar costs too much to risk having such a large batch as a kettleful spoiled. We boil it by the thermometer, and when it is at just the right point we take it off and put it into these coolers, where it thickens and is reduced to a workable temperature. That which is to be used as filling is then shifted into these big cylindrical cans that have inside them a series of revolving fingers and here the candy is beaten until quite smooth; whatever flavoring or coloring matter is needed is beaten into it."

As the machinery whirled the boys stood watching the beaters.

"Some of this beaten sugar will be colored pink, flavored with rose or wintergreen, and used for the centers of chocolate; some will have maple flavoring, some vanilla, some lemon. Nuts will be stirred into some of the rest of it. There is an almost endless number of ways in which it may be varied. Come over here and see them preparing the centers and getting them ready to cover with chocolate."

It was an interesting process.

Shallow wooden trays filled with dry corn-starch passed beneath a machine which left in them rows of empty holes the size of the heart of a chocolate cream. The trays then moved on until they stopped just under a nozzle, which ran exactly the right amount of liquid filling into each hole. The dryness of the corn-starch prevented the mixture from flowing together. As soon as every hole in the tray was filled with fondant it was set away to cool and an empty tray substituted. When the little centers were hard enough they were taken out of the corn-starch moulds, and after being put upon traveling strips of fine wire netting, melted chocolate was poured over them. The wire frames sped along like miniature moving sidewalks, their contents drying and cooling on the way. In the meantime the superfluous chocolate dripped through the netting into a trough beneath and was collected to be melted over again. On went the finished chocolates until they reached the packing-room, where girls removed them from the frames, sorted them, and put them into boxes.

"These are not what is known as hand-dipped or fork-dipped chocolates," explained the boy. "Those are higher priced, because they require individual attention, and the material put into them is more expensive. To make those the girls take the centers and submerge each one in melted chocolate with a dipping-fork, finishing the pieces with a certain little twist or decoration on top; it requires no small amount of skill to make this top-knot, which not only serves to render the candy more attractive but to distinguish one variety of filling from another. Each kind has its own particular decoration. After some practice any of us might, I suppose, learn to make the twist on a chocolate once; but to make that precise thing each time and never vary it would be quite a different matter. It is important the pattern should be uniform, since both the dippers and the packers must know what is inside; in addition those who sell the candy must know. It is no easy task. After the chocolates are finished *Eureka* is stamped on the bottom of every piece and they are ready to be sold."

"I don't see what prevents your candy from sticking to everything," observed Van thoughtfully.

[Illustration: "IT IS NO EASY TASK"]

"Blasts of cool air that come through those overhead pipes. We can turn on the current whenever we wish. Whenever the girls who are packing candy find that it is becoming soft they turn on a current of cold air to chill and harden it; we often use these cool blasts, too, when handling candies in the process of making. Such kinds as butter-scotch, hoarhound, and the pretty twisted varieties stick together very easily. If they are allowed to become lumpy or marred they are useless for the trade and have to be melted over."

"What are those men over there doing?" inquired Bob, pointing to a group of workmen who were stirring a seething mixture of nuts and molasses.

"Some of them are making peanut brittle, some caramels; and in the last kettle I believe they are boiling hoarhound candy. See! The last man is ready to empty his upon the table. Suppose we go over and watch him."

They reached the spot just in time to see the kettle lifted and the hot candy poured out upon the metal top of the table, where it spread itself like a small, irregular pond. At once the workman in charge took up a steel bar not unlike a metal yardstick and began pressing down the mass to a uniform thickness. This done he ran the bar deftly beneath and turned the vast piece over just as one would flop over some gigantic griddle-cake. He continued to change it from side to side, pressing it down in any spot where it was too thick, but never once touching it with his hands. He then cut off a long narrow strip and fed it into a machine at his elbow, the boys regarding him expectantly. Suddenly, to their great surprise, the formless ribbon of candy that had gone into the machine began to come forth at the other end in prettily marked discs, each with the firm name stamped upon it.

"Hoarhound tablets, you see," observed the boy. "The Italian who is making peanut brittle has flattened his on the table in the same fashion and marked it into bars which later will be cut and wrapped in paraffine paper."

"I never realized so much candy was manufactured in one day," exclaimed Bob as they went down in the elevator.

"Oh, this isn't much," returned the boy. "We are running light just now. You should come a few weeks before Christmas if you want to see things hum here."

"I guess that would be a good time for visitors to keep out," returned Bob as they smilingly bade good-bye to their guide and started home in the motor-car.

As the automobile glided into Fifth Avenue Van said:

"Look, Bobbie, there's a candy shop! I suppose all that stuff in the window was made in exactly the same way as those things we saw to-day don't you?"

But Bob did not turn his head.

Instead he replied:

"Don't say candy to me. I do not want to lay eyes on another piece of it for a week!"

"Nor I!" Van echoed. "Do you wonder that boy at the factory feels as he does? I guess your father can keep his money so far as we are concerned. He'll have no candy bills from us."

* * * * *

In the meantime Mr. Carlton waited for the tremendous bonbon bill that had threatened to reduce his bank account, and when it was not forthcoming he nodded his head and chuckled quietly to himself.

CHAPTER VIII

VAN MUTINIES

Another day passed and Bob and Van were once more back at Colversham greeting the boys and vainly endeavoring to settle down to the work of the last term.

"It seems as if the stretch from April to June is about the hardest pull of the whole year," yawned Van, looking up for the twentieth time from his Latin lesson and gazing out into the sunny campus. "Studying is bad enough at best, but when the trout brooks begin to run and the canoeing is good it is a deadly proposition to be cooped up in this room hammering away for the finals."

"It always seems worse after a vacation," agreed Bob, tilting back in his chair. "You'll get back into the harness, though, in a day or two; you know you always yap just about so much when you first get back to school."

"I don't yap, as you call it, any worse than most fellows do. I hate being tied up like a pup on a leash. It seems as if I'd just have to get out and play ball--and if you were a human being you'd want to, too," growled Van.

"Hang it all, don't you suppose I want to?" Bob retorted. "What do you think I'm made of, anyway?"

"I don't know, Bobbie. Sometimes you're so resigned I begin to fear you are a mummy," was Van's laughing retort. "Now, I'm not like that It is one big grind for me to study. The minute spring comes it seems as if I never could translate another line of Cicero as long as I lived, and I don't care a hurray what X equals. What will it matter a hundred years hence whether we plug away here at this stuff, or get out and play ball?"

"I guess you'd find it would matter to you right now without waiting for the end of a century," was the laconic answer. "But speaking of ball, what wouldn't you give to see the first League game of the season in town, Saturday? That will be some playing!"

"I clean forgot the season opened this week," exclaimed Van. "Since I got back here I've been all mixed up on dates. I thought it was next week. Are you sure it's Saturday?"

Bob nodded.

"Positive."

"It'll be a cracker-jack game," mused Van. "I'd give something to be there. You don't suppose we could get off at noon and go, do you?"

"Not on your life! Right now, after vacation? What do you take this school faculty for--an entertainment committee? You seem to forget we'd have to cut algebra, and English, and gym."

"I shouldn't care."

"I should. I'm working this trip, and can't afford to miss recitations," was Bob's sharp reply. "As for you, you can afford to miss them even less than I can--you know that. Put it out of your head. When you can't do a thing there is no use thinking about it and wishing you could."

"I see no earthly harm in talking about it."

"I do. It just keeps you stirred up."

"Then what did you mention it for in the beginning?"

"I don't know. I wish to goodness I hadn't," Bob declared.

"Well, in spite of your opinions I repeat I'd give a fiver to see that game Saturday."

"You can't, so cut it out and let me finish this theme. Every time I've started to write you've broken in and driven every blooming idea out of my head. Now quit it. You better pitch into your own work for to-morrow. Dig out all the Cicero you can, and later I'll help you with the rest."

With finality Bob wheeled his chair around and proceeded to submerge himself in his task.

But not so Van. He took up his book, to be sure, but over the top of it his eyes roved to the world outside, and fixed themselves dreamily on the line of hills that peeped above the tips of the red maples budding in the school campus. He was far away from Colversham and its round of duties. In imagination he moved with a gay, eager crowd through the gateway leading into the great city ball ground. He could hear the game called; watch the first swirl of the ball as it curved from the pitcher's hand; catch the sharp click of the bat against it; and join in the roar of applause as the swift-footed runner sped to second base.

Everybody would be at that opening game!

Not to go when it was within trolley distance was absurd.

What was algebra, English, or a little wall-scaling compared to such an opportunity?

And, anyway, who would be the wiser?

There must be ways of getting off so nobody, not even Bob, would know.

If only Bob could be persuaded to cut school!

But it was never any use to urge Bob when he spoke in that horribly positive tone. You might just as well try to move a lighthouse.

Van glanced furtively at his chum who, unconscious of his scrutiny, was writing steadily down a long page of foolscap. The sight had a steadying effect. Van again took up his book and scowled once more at that same old line at the top of the page. But all the time between his eyes and his Latin lesson swayed that alluring throng of pleasure seekers. Impatiently he tried to banish them, but stern as was his attempt their laughter still sounded in his ears. Against his will he was back at the ball game, and this time he was on his feet shouting wildly with the other fans as Carruth, the star batter, made a soaring hit and stole two bases on it. In that instant of unreined enthusiasm Van Blake decided that come what might he would go to the game on Saturday--go even though his whole term's work went for naught.

The resolve made he tried to stifle his conscience by falling upon his Latin with unwonted zeal, and so ardently did he wrestle with it that when, an hour later, Bob pushed aside his papers and offered to help him with the lesson he was able to greet his chum with a translation so far beyond his customary efforts that Bob patted him on the head with paternal pride, exclaiming:

"Bully for you, old man! That's about the best work I ever knew of your doing. The middle of it is a little queer, but we'll fix that up all right. Who says you're not a Cicero?"

"Bobbie, if I thought for one moment that there was any danger of my becoming a Cicero or any other Latin worthy I'd go drown myself!" Van cried, startled at the mere thought. "I'm not so worse, though, am I? I'd no idea I could reel it off like that."

"Of course you can do it. Why, Van, you could do all kinds of things if you'd only go at them. The trouble with you is that you always study with one eye out the window. If you'd only get down to your job with all your might you'd not only get your lessons better but you'd learn them in half the time."

"I 'spect that's so," drawled Van lazily. "I ought to duff right in on all fours. I acknowledge it. But it is not so easy to make your mind go where you send it."

He broke off, shifting the subject to athletics, and was in the highest spirits the rest of the day; but underneath all his fun and banter the question constantly arose in his inner consciousness: How could he elude his roommate's watchfulness and on the coming Saturday escape to the great game?

Strangely enough Fortune seemed to smile upon his plot, for Friday morning Bob was taken to the infirmary with a sore throat, which, although slight, isolated him from the rest of the boys. No longer was he at Van's elbow to watch, warn, or censure.

The coast was entirely clear.

Van formulated his plans.

Directly after luncheon on Saturday he would start for the city, hugging the edge of the campus and afterward cutting across the adjoining estate to meet the car line where it forked into the main road. Many another boy had done the same and not been caught; why not he? It was, to be sure, against the rules to leave the school grounds without permission, but one must take a chance now and then. Did not half the spice of life lay in risks?

Accordingly after the noonday meal was finished and the boys had scattered to recitations or the dormitories Van sauntered idly out past the tennis-courts; across the field skirting the golf course and then with one sudden plunge was behind the gymnasium and running like a deer for the thicket that separated Colversham from the Sawyer estate. He knew the lay of the land perfectly, for this short cut was a favorite thoroughfare of the boys, in spite of the posted protest of *No Trespassing*.

Creeping cautiously through the shelter of the orchard he contrived to escape observation and reach the highway in safety; at this quiet noon hour the road was entirely deserted save for the presence of one small boy who was jogging on ahead, a dinner pail upon his arm. He was a slender little fellow of six or seven years who whistled shrilly as he went and kicked up clouds of dust with his bare feet. As Van watched the sway of his shoulders and the unhampered tread of his unshod feet he could not but recall the days when he, too, had gloried in going barefoot. He smiled at the memory which now seemed so absurd.

A slight sound behind him broke in upon his reverie.

Bounding the turn just at his back swept a big scarlet touring-car driven by a solitary man. It was coming at tremendous speed and no horn had given warning of its noiseless approach. Van had but an instant to step out of its path when on it shot, bearing down on the unconscious boy ahead. The little chap was walking in the middle of the road and whistling so loudly that no hint of the oncoming danger reached him. The man in the motor saw the child and sounding his horn, swerved to the left; but it was too late. The speeding car caught the lad, struck him, and tossed him to the roadside rushing on in its mad flight faster, if anything, than before.

In vain did Van call after it.

His protest was useless.

The great red vehicle whirled forward, a speck in the sunshine, and was lost to view.

Terror-stricken Van darted to the child's side and bent over him.

His eyes were closed and an ugly gash in his forehead was bleeding profusely.

[Illustration: NO HORN HAD GIVEN WARNING]

Binding a handkerchief round the little fellow's head the older boy lifted him in his arms and retracing his steps ran with him down the road, across the Sawyer lawn, and up the steps of the Colversham infirmary.

A young orderly who was lounging at the door came forward and on seeing the child's face spoke quickly to a physician who was passing through the hall. Together they took the little boy from Van's arms and carried him to a cot in an adjoining room, anxiously plying Van with questions as they went.

Briefly Van related the story.

"Such men should be hung! Prison is too good for them!" snapped the doctor angrily.

He passed his hand with infinite tenderness over the tiny, still form on the bed.

"Is he much hurt, sir?" questioned Van eagerly.

"I can't tell yet. He is hurt enough so that he doesn't come to his senses, poor little chap! Here, Jackson, ring for a couple of nurses. We'll get the child upstairs."

Van tagged behind them more because he was anxious to hear of the lad's condition than because he could be of any real use.

As the sad procession left the elevator, emerging into the corridor on the second floor, a tall man who was coming down the stairway confronted them.

It was Dr. Maitland, the principal of the school!

"What's this?" he asked, advancing with swift stride.

The doctor hurriedly explained the circumstances.

"A motor accident on the Claybrook Road, you say? Well, well! Poor little chap! Who brought him in?"

"This lad--one of the schoolboys. You showed good judgment, Blake, and it was a mighty fortunate thing that you were there," observed the surgeon, passing on.

"The Claybrook Road?" repeated the puzzled principal. "You were on the Claybrook Road, Blake? And what were you doing there at this time of day?"

With throbbing heart Van suddenly came to himself.

Up to that instant no thought of his own peculiar plight had crossed his mind. Now the reality of his dilemma rushed upon him with pitiless force.

"May I ask," repeated the principal in measured tone, "what were you doing on the Claybrook Road at this hour, Blake?"

CHAPTER IX

VAN'S GREAT DEED

Dr Maitland, who was a man of unswerving justice, was influenced in his judgments neither by pity nor explanations, and thus it came about that when Van had answered his questions, putting before him the facts about his runaway, the principal sent the boy to his own room to there await sentence Van was in the lowest of spirits. What would the penalty of his insurrection be? He knew Dr. Maitland far too well to expect mercy, nor did he wish it. He was too proud for that. He had disobeyed the rules of the school, and he must now bear the punishment, be it what it would. The thought of holding back the facts had never entered his mind. Indolent he sometimes was even to laziness but never within his memory had he been dishonest. So he had fearlessly told the truth, and despite the calamity it threatened he found himself the happier for telling it. Whether it would mean expulsion from Colversham he did not know; probably it would.

To think of leaving Colversham, the place he loved so much! And in disgrace, too. What would the other boys say? And his father?

Van shrank at the thought of telling his father.

Mr. Blake was a severe man who, like Dr. Maitland, would not gloss over the affair either by tolerance or sympathy. He would be angry, and he would have the right to be. Van admitted that. As he looked back on his school days he realized for the first time how indulgent his father had been; he had denied his son no reasonable wish, simply asking in return that the boy express his gratitude by studiousness and obedience. Van flushed as with vividness it came to his consciousness that he had repaid his father's goodness with neither of these things. He had studied just as little as was possible, and in place of appreciation he had rendered nothing but disgrace.

His self-esteem was at a very low ebb when Bob, dismissed from the infirmary, returned to his old quarters. Van was seldom depressed--so seldom, in fact, that the sight aroused in his chum nothing but an anxiety lest he be ill. Surely nothing but sickness could cause Van Blake to lie on a couch, his face buried in pillows!

"What's the matter, old fellow?" called Bob the instant he was inside the door. "Are you used up?"

No answer.

"I say, what's the trouble?" Bob repeated, hurrying to his side.

It took much questioning before the story could be drawn from the boy's reluctant lips.

"When Bob had at last heard it he was silent.

"Can't you say something?" queried Van peevishly.

"I hardly know what to say," Bob answered with slow gentleness. "I'm so sorry--so sorry and upset. I can't for the life of me understand how you came to do such a thing. Did you expect to get away with it? You must have known you would be missed at recitations and tracked down."

"That's right--rub it in!"

"I'm not rubbing it in; I'm only trying to understand it."

"There's nothing to understand. I just was crazy to go to that ball game and I started. I should have gone, too, if it hadn't been for the kid getting hurt."

"It was bully of you to bring him back, anyway," Bob said. "Of course you knew it was all up with you when you did it."

"I didn't think about it at all. I wasn't thinking of anything but that poor little chap who was mowed down by the brute in that car. If I hadn't happened to hear the motor it might have been me instead. I wish it had been," he declared gloomily.

"No you don't. Great Scott, cheer up, Van! The country hasn't gone to the dogs yet. I must admit you are in a mess; but it doesn't begin to be the mess it would have been if you had gone to the game, had a bang-up time, and come home a sneak who had stolen his fun. At least you have done the square thing and 'fessed up, and now you'll be man enough to take what's coming to you. What do you suppose Maitland will do?"

"I can guess pretty well--pack me off home. He is stiff as a ramrod on obedience to the school rules," sighed Van, "and he's right, too. It is perfectly fair. I knew it when I went."

"I can't see, just for one afternoon of sport, how you--" Bob broke off. "If I'd only been here you never would have gone."

"Maybe not," admitted Van. Then he added in the same breath: "No, I shouldn't have gone if you had been here, Bobbie. Somehow you're my good angel. I wrote Father so the other day."

"Stuff!"

"It's true. You are such a brick! I thought you'd blow my head off when you'd heard what I'd done."

"Well, I am mad enough to do it," was the tart reply. "For you to go and do a thing like that just for a ball game! It wasn't worth it. Think of your being pitched out of Colversham for a measly game of baseball. And you didn't get there, either!"

Van kicked the pillows impatiently.

"Don't light into me, Bobbie," he moaned. "Don't I feel bad enough as it is?"

"I don't know whether you do or not; you ought to."

"I do, Bob. I'm dead sorry."

"If you'd stay sorry it might do some good," returned Bob. A sudden thought seemed to strike him. He did not speak for a few moments; then he said half aloud: "Who knows--it might help."

"What might help?"

"Nothing."

Bob got up and sauntered to the door.

"Will you stay right here like a decent chap and not get into any more mischief until I get back?"

"Where are you going?"

"Nowhere much--just across the campus for a little while. I'll be back soon. Will you wait here exactly where you are?"

"Yes, but--"

"Honor bright?"

"Sure!"

"All right. Don't quit this room until I come. So long!"

Bob was gone.

Van lay very still after the door had closed, and to keep him company in his solitude back swarmed all those dreary thoughts that Bob's cheery presence had for the time being banished; with a rush they came to jeer, taunt, and terrify.

The *little while* lengthened into an hour and on into a second one.

The room became intolerable.

Then upon the stone floor of the corridor outside sounded Bob's foot.

"Still here, Van?" he cried, coming in with elastic step and banging the door after him.

His face was wreathed in smiles.

"What's happened to you that you look like that?" questioned Van, sitting up among the pillows.

"Like what?"

"Why, as if somebody had sent you a Christmas-tree or made you president of a railroad?"

Bob laughed.

"I've been to see the Head," he said.

"Humph! I never knew of his causing any one such overwhelming delight," observed Van a little spitefully.

"Hush up, old man; don't run down the Doctor," Bob said. "You may have more cause to be grateful to him than you know."

"You don't mean--" Van's voice trembled. "Did you go to see him about me?"

Bob nodded.

"Bob! How did you dare?"

"I dare do anything that becomes a man; who dares do more is none," quoted Bob merrily. "I don't believe, though, I'd have dared go for myself," he answered. "It is different when you are doing it for some one else. Now sit up and listen and I'll tell you all about it. The Doctor was mighty white about you; but in spite of all he stuck to the fact that you'd disobeyed the rules; he kept going back to that every time I tried to switch him off. We squabbled over you a solid hour, and the upshot of it was this: you are to stay at Colversham--"

"Hurrah!"

Van hurled a pillow into the air.

"Shut up and hear the rest of it. You are to stay here because I promised upon my word of honor that you would keep straight and study."

"I'll do it."

"That isn't all."

Bob hesitated.

It was a wrench for him to deliver the remainder of the message.

"Yes, you are to stay," he repeated as if to gain time. "But of course you can't expect to slip through with no punishment at all."

"No, indeed!"

Still Van spoke with jaunty hopefulness.

"The Doctor thinks it is only fair that you should be pretty severely reminded of what you've done."

"That's all right. I'm not afraid. Fire ahead! What's he going to do with me?"

"He thinks--he says--he feels it is best--"

"Oh, come on, come on--out with it!"

"He has forbidden you to take any part in the school athletics this spring," was the reluctant whisper.

Van did not speak.

"I'm mighty sorry, old fellow," declared Bob, "but it was the best I could do."

Still Van made no reply.

With troubled gaze Bob regarded his chum.

"I'd far rather Maitland had knocked me out," he ventured at last.

Stooping, he put his hand on Van's shoulder.

Van roused himself and looked up into his friend's face with one of his quick smiles.

"It's all right, Bob," he said. "Don't you fuss about me any more. You were a trump to get me off as well as you did. I'll take my medicine without whimpering. I ought to bless my stars that my banishment from athletics is only temporary. Suppose I had been smashed up so I could never play another game like that little kid, Tim McGrew," he shuddered. "It was just sheer luck that saved me. Why, do you suppose, he should have been the one to be crippled and I go scot free?" he observed meditatively.

"I don't know. Maybe because there is something in the world that only you can do. My father believes that."

"Do you?"

"I don't know."

"It would be strange, wouldn't it, to feel you were let off just to do something?" mused Van. "You'd be wondering all the time what it was. Of course it would be something big."

"You could never tell what it was," Bob replied, falling in with his friend's mood. "I suppose the only way to make sure would be to do whatever came to you the best way you could do it. You never could be sure that what you were doing was not the great thing."

"Not studying and stuff like that."

"It might be; or at least studying might lead to it."

"I don't believe it."

"It wouldn't hurt you to try it."

"No, I suppose not." Then with characteristic caprice Van shifted the subject. "But seriously, Bobbie, there is something I am going to do. You'll howl, I guess, and maybe you'll be disappointed, too. It's about that sick kid, Tim McGrew. The surgeon says the little beggar will never walk again. I feel pretty sore about it; I suppose because I was there," explained Van uneasily. "I've about decided to chip in the money Father was going to send me for a canoe and get a wheel chair for him. His folks are poor, and can't get one, and the doctor says--"

"You're a--"

"Oh, shut up, can't you, Bobbie? It's only because I'm so cut up about the accident. Remember, it might have been me instead of him. You won't mind much if we don't have the canoe, will you?"

"No," was the low answer.

Neither of the boys spoke for some time.

Then Bob whispered:

"Have you thought, Van, that maybe the thing you are to do is something for that little lame boy, Tim McGrew?"

CHAPTER X

HOW VAN BORE HIS PUNISHMENT

The spring term passed much faster than either Bob or Van dreamed it would and despite the absence of athletics Van Blake found plenty to do to fill the gap left by this customary activity.

In the first place there was his studying. Had not Bob assumed an obligation that must be lived up to and that was quite as binding as if it existed on paper instead of in a mere invisible point of honor? He was very grateful to Bob and had given bond that he would live up to the pledge his chum had made for him. Now he must fulfil his promise, Van argued. So although the call of the springtime was strong and difficult to resist he had been faithful to his work, "plugging away," as he expressed it, with all his strength. To his surprise the task, so irksome at first, became interesting. It was a novel experience to enter a classroom and instead of moving in a mental haze possess a clear idea of what was going on. Twice he was able to furnish the correct answers to Latin questions on which every one else had failed, and what a thrill of satisfaction accompanied the performance!

The attitude of his teachers changed, too. Formerly they had been polite; now they became even cordial, demonstrating by an unsuspected friendliness that they were after all ordinary human beings and rather likable ones at that. They were moreover amazingly sympathetic and met every endeavor of Van's with generous aid. Perhaps schools were not the prison-houses he had formerly thought them!

There had, of course, been no chance to conceal from the boys the reason of his banishment from the ball field and tennis-courts; such a story as the motor accident travels with insidious speed. Before a day had passed from one end of Colversham to the other everybody knew that Van Blake had disobeyed the school rules and had in consequence forfeited his place in out-of-door sports. Van, however, was a great favorite and the manly way in which he accepted his penalty provoked nothing but admiration and respect from his classmates. He frankly admitted his mistake, owning that while his sentence was severe it was perfectly just; nor would he permit a word of criticism of Dr. Maitland's decree to be voiced in his hearing.

"Maitland is all right!" was his hearty endorsement, and that remark was the only encouragement his pals received when they came to condone with him.

Gradually the affair dropped out of sight. Van went among the boys, cheerily giving advice as to the make-up of the school teams and even coaching the fellow who was to serve as his successor as pitcher on the line.

Nevertheless there still remained quite a margin of leisure, and it was during this lonely interval when every one else was training for the coming games that he would stray off by himself and visit little Tim McGrew. Between the two a peculiar friendship sprang up. On Van's part it arose from forlornness mingled with a half formulated belief that he must do something to express his thankfulness that he himself had escaped from the fate that had overtaken the child. On the small lad's side it had its root in gratitude and hero-worship. In Tim's eyes Van Blake was an all-powerful person. Was it not he who had picked him up and carried him to the hospital? And had not this same big schoolboy bought the beautiful wheel-chair that enabled one to travel about the house and yard almost as readily as if on foot? In addition to all this was it not Van who came often to the house, never forgetting to bring in his pocket some toy or picture-book? Small things they often were--these gifts that meant so much to the child--often things of very slight money value; but to the invalid whose long, tedious days of convalescence were stretches of monotony the tiny presents seemed treasures from an enchanted land.

Tim was now at home in the shabby cottage on the outskirts of Colversham where he lived with his mother and four sisters. Poor as the place was it was spotlessly neat and Tim's family were spotlessly tidy too. Mrs. McGrew, who supported her household by doing washing for some of the families in the town, might have had a permanent and much more lucrative position elsewhere had it not been for leaving her five little ones; as it was, she clung to her children, struggling to meet her living expenses as best she could. It had been a sore grief to her when Tim, her only boy and the baby of the home, had become crippled. Perhaps she sensed more clearly than did the lad the full seriousness of the calamity. As for Tim, he accepted it in childish fashion, hopefully ignoring the problems of the future.

To Van Blake Mrs. McGrew was all gratitude. Of all her children her boy was her favorite.

"But for you, sir, little Timmie might have been left at the roadside to die," she would exclaim over and over. "We'll never forget it--never--neither I nor the children!"

It was thus that Van became the hero of the McGrew household, and the warmth and genuineness of the welcome he unfailingly received there aroused in him an answering friendliness. Many a time when he saw things either new or interesting he would find himself instinctively saying:

"I must tell Tim about that," or "I must take that to Tim."

But with his enthronement as the sovereign of Tim's universe there came to Van a very disquieting experience. Tim thought his big friend knew everything, and in consequence whenever he became puzzled about facts that were being read to him or that he heard he would instantly appeal to Van, whom he was sure could right every sort of dilemma that might arise. But too often the unlucky Van was forced to blush and falter that he would have to look it up; and when he did so he frequently learned something himself. For Tim never forgot. No sooner would Van be inside the gate than the shrill little voice would pipe: "And did you find out how far away Mars is, Mr. Blake?"

Poor Van, it kept him scrambling to satisfy Tim McGrew's intellectual curiosity, yet there was a tang in the game that rendered it very interesting. He found, too, ample reward in seeing the wee invalid's face brighten when the query was answered.

So the spring sped on.

In the meantime Van had heard only irregularly from his parents. In a long letter to his father he had sent all the facts of his disgrace at school and had added that he was truly sorry; the reply he received had been terse and rather stern but not unkind. Mr. Blake expressed much regret for his son's conduct and closed his epistle with the caustic comment that he should look for a proof of Van's desire to make good. That was all. Van knew that Dr. Maitland had also written; but what he did not know was that with the fearlessness so characteristic of him Bob Carlton had taken the time and trouble to pen a long note to Colorado as a plea for his chum. It was a remarkable composition from a boy so young--a letter full of affection and earnestness and voicing a surprising insight into his friend's character and disposition. Mr. Blake read it over three times, and when he finished sat in a reverie with it still between his fingers. The tone of it was so like the man he had known long ago, that friend from whom a misunderstanding that now seemed pitiably trivial had separated him. It had been his fault; Mr. Blake could see that now. He had been both hasty and unjust. Over him surged a great wave of regret. Well, it was too late to mend the matter at this late day. One chance was, however, left him--to make up to the son for the injustice done the father.

It therefore came about that at the close of the school term Bob Carlton was overjoyed to receive from Van's parents an invitation to come west with their boy and pass the summer holidays. Such a miracle seemed too good to be a reality, and the lads' instant fear was that the Carltons would be unwilling to spare Bob from home for such a long time. To their surprise, however, Mr. Carlton welcomed the plan with enthusiasm. A trip to Colorado would be a wonderful opportunity, the educational value of which could scarcely be estimated, he argued. Underneath this most excellent reason there also existed on Mr. Carlton's part a desire to show his former partner that he cherished no ill will for the past. Who knew but the boy might even be a messenger of peace?

So one June morning, after bidding good-bye to Colversham and to Tim McGrew, the two lads set forth on their western journey. They were in high spirits. Both had passed the examinations with honors, and as Van thought of his achievement again and again he wondered if it could be true that he was one of that light-hearted band who were starting off on their summer vacation with no conditions to work off.

The solitary cloud on the horizon was the grief of little Tim at having his friend go. But Van promised there should be letters--lots of them--and post-cards, too, all along the route; the parting would not be for long anyway.

These were some of the thoughts that surged through Van's mind as he and Bob settled themselves into their places on the train and began the attempt to fathom the reams of directions Mr. Blake had sent them; pages and pages there were of what to do and what not to do on the long trip, the letter closing with the single sentence:

"I am trusting you to make this journey alone because I believe your chum, Bob Carlton, has a level head."

"If your own head is not level, Bobbie, it is at least an honor to be associated with a head that is," remarked Van humorously. "I guess that is about all the recommendation you need from Dad, old boy. I wonder how he happened to take such a fancy to you without ever having met you."

"I wonder," echoed Bob quietly.

CHAPTER XI

THE BOYS MAKE A NEW ACQUAINTANCE

To Bob every mile of the western journey was a step into Wonderland; novel sights, novel ideas confronted him on every hand and viewed through the medium of his enthusiasm things that had become threadbare to Van became, as if by magic, suddenly new. The greatness of the country was a marvel of which Bob had never before had any adequate conception. Then there were the cities, alive with varying industries, and teeming with their strangely mixed American population. Above all was the amazing natural beauty of scenery hitherto undreamed of. Hour after hour Bob sat spellbound at the window of the observation-car, never tiring of watching the shifting landscape as it whirled past. His interest and intelligence caught the notice of a gentleman who occupied the section opposite the boys, and soon the three formed one of those pleasant acquaintances so frequently made in traveling.

Mr. Powers (for that was the stranger's name) was on his way back to his farm in Utah, and very eager was he to reach home.

"So many things on the place need my attention that the journey you are delighting in seems very long to me," he remarked to Bob one morning as they came from the dining-car.

"Is your farm a large one, Mr. Powers?" questioned Bob.

Mr. Powers smiled.

"It is larger than you would want to build a fence around," he returned humorously.

"I suppose you have all sorts of cows and pigs and horses on it, and raise every kind of fruit and vegetable that ever was invented," put in Van mischievously.

Mr. Powers shook his head and looked not a little amused.

"No. We have only enough stock for our own use--nothing fancy. I do not go in for show farming. I raise only one thing on my land, and I'm going to see if you are clever enough to guess what it is."

"Alfalfa!" cried Bob instantly.

"No. How did you happen to think of that?"

"Oh, I've read that lots of western farmers raised it."

"True enough. It wasn't a bad guess, but it was not the right one," said the stranger. "Now suppose we hear from your chum."

"Corn."

"Still wrong; but you are getting warmer."

"Wheat."

"Wheat is not as good a random shot as corn."

"It must be a vegetable," declared Bob thoughtfully. "Let me see. Not potatoes?"

"No."

"Of course it couldn't be peas, or beans, or squash, because you said once you had hundreds of acres, and you would never raise any of those things in such large quantities," argued Van. "Spinach, tomatoes--"

"I have it!" cried Bob. "You should have guessed it the first thing, Van."

"Why?"

"Can't you think? With your father right in the business you ought to."

"Beets," exclaimed Van.

"Beets it is!" agreed Mr. Powers. "So your father is interested in beets too, is he? You don't chance to be the son of Mr. Asa Blake, do you?"

"Yes, sir."

"That is a coincidence," observed Mr. Powers much interested. "I sell all my crops to him. I expect then, young man, you know all there is to be known about growing beets."

"On the contrary, I don't know a thing," Van confessed laughing. "Dad has never talked to me much about his business. He is too busy to talk to anybody," he added a little dubiously.

"It is usually the doctor's children who never get any medicine," chuckled Mr. Powers. "Now, I could do better than that for you. I could tell you considerable about beets if you urged me to."

"I wish you would," answered the boys promptly.

"There, you see, you urge me at once--you insist upon hearing! What can I do? There is no escape for me but to comply with your request. Of course I was not expecting to be called upon to speak to-day and therefore I must crave the indulgence of the audience if I am but poorly prepared," began Mr. Powers with mock gravity.

"In the first place you must remember that while sugar-cane can only be cultivated in a hot, moist climate, beets grow best in the temperate zone. In the United States there is a belt of beet-sugar land two hundred miles wide that runs irregularly across the country from southern New England to the Pacific coast. Sugar-beets can, of course, be grown elsewhere, but it is in this particular region that they thrive best. If even a small proportion of this area were to be planted with beets we could get enough sugar from them to enable us to ship it to foreign markets instead of yearly importing a large amount of it. The trouble is that we Americans are so rich in land that we waste it and fail to get from it a tenth part of what we might. If you doubt that travel in Europe and see what is done with land on the other side; or, better yet, watch what some Italian in this country will get from a bit of land no bigger than your pocket handkerchief."

Mr. Powers stopped a minute and looked out of the window.

"The great objection our people make to growing beets is that they injure the soil so that nothing else planted afterward will flourish. Now to an extent this is true. Beets do run out the soil if they are raised year after year on the same land. If our farmers were not so slow to get a new idea they would raise beets in rotation as is done in Europe."

"What do you mean by rotation?" demanded Bob.

"A rotating crop is one that produces a sequence of different kinds of harvests," explained Mr. Powers. "By that I mean harvests of entirely varying nature.

Abroad they have learned that a hoed crop, when planted annually, destroys the productivity of the earth; therefore foreigners plant beets one year in three or five and cereals, turnips, or something else in between times. Formerly they used to let the land lie fallow a year to rest it, but now they have worked out a scheme by which they get a crop every year. It was Napoleon, that Frenchman of wonderful brain, who first discovered the value of beets for making sugar, and thought out the plan for raising them in rotation with other varieties of crops. He commanded that ninety thousand acres of beets be planted in different parts of France, and he established in connection with this decree a great fund of money from which bonuses were to be paid to persons who built factories to manufacture beet-sugar. He went even further, furnishing free instruction to all who wished to learn the industry. In consequence at the end of a couple of years there were in France over three hundred small sugar factories; little by little this number has increased until now the sugar product of the French nation is enormous."

Fascinated by the story Bob and Van listened attentively.

"Didn't other countries steal the idea of the rotating crop?" inquired Van.

"Not at first. Germany tried to make her farmers believe in the new notion, but failed," answered Mr. Powers. "Later, however, as an inducement, the German government helped beet-sugar factories pay such good prices for beets that the farmers became anxious to raise them; at the same time a high duty was placed on imported sugar, and the result was that the German people were forced to manufacture their own. At the present time about one-half of the sugar used by all the world is made in foreign factories. I myself run my beet farm on the rotation principle, and find that the hoed root crops seem to stimulate the others; but I can't convince my neighbors of it."

"Does beet-sugar taste any different from cane?" inquired Bob.

"Not a whit; you couldn't tell the difference," was Mr. Powers' answer.

"I suppose sugar-beets are just like those in our gardens," ventured Van.

"No, they're not; they are, however, not unlike them. They differ in having more juice and in usually being white," replied Mr. Powers. "The ground has first to be plowed and harrowed, and is afterward laid off in eighteen-inch rows because beets, you know, are planted from seed. When the crop comes up trouble begins, for it has to be thinned until each plant has a good area in which to grow; the beets must also be carefully weeded and the soil round them loosened if they are to thrive."

"How long is it before they are ready for sugar making?" inquired Bob.

"Practically five months; it depends somewhat on the season. When they are ripe they are dug up, the tops are removed, and they are floated down small canals where washing machines with revolving brushes remove from them every atom of dirt."

"And then?"

"If they are to be made directly into syrup and do not have to be shipped in bulk they go into slicers which cut them into V-shaped pieces about the length and thickness of a slate pencil, these pieces being called cossettes. The sliced beet-root is next put into warm water tanks in order that the sugar contained in it may be drawn out. Built in a circle, these tanks are connected, and as the beets move from one vat to another more and more sugar is taken from them until they reach the last vat when the beet pulp is of no further use except to be used as fodder for live stock. The juice remains in the tanks, and in color it is--"

"Red!" cried Van, thoughtlessly interrupting.

"No, son, not red. It is black as ink."

"Black!" exclaimed the boys in a chorus.

"Black as your shoe."

"But--but I don't see how they--" Van stopped, bewildered.

"They bleach it by injecting fumes of sulphur gas into the tanks; lime is also used to--"

"To clear it after the dirt has come to the top," put in the boys in a breath.

"Exactly so," laughed Mr. Powers. "I observe you are now at the home plate."

[Illustration: "THESE TANKS ARE CONNECTED"]

"We saw it done at the sugar-cane refinery," explained Bob.

"I see," nodded Mr. Powers. "Well, the principle of making beet-sugar is the same as cane-sugar. By the use of chemical solutions the juice is cleared until it is perfectly white."

Bob nudged Van with his elbow and the lads smiled understandingly. There was no danger of their forgetting Mr. Hennessey and his secret chemical formula.

"The remainder of the process is also similar to that used in refining cane-sugar. The syrup passes from tank to tank, constantly thickening, and the molasses is extracted in the same fashion by being thrown off in the centrifugal machines when the sugar crystallizes. Molasses is often boiled two and three times to make second and third grade molasses for the trade, and you must remember in this connection that the names *New Orleans* and *Porto Rico* do not necessarily indicate where the product was made, but rather its quality, these varieties being of the finest grade."

Mr. Powers rose and drew out a cigar.

"I think I'm quite a lecturer, don't you?" he said. "I imagine your father, Van, could have told you this story much better than I have if you could have captured him for two hours on a train when he had nothing else to do. As it is I have had to fill his place, and I want you to inform him with my compliments that I am surprised to discover how completely he has neglected his son's education."

With a mischievous twinkle in his eye Mr. Powers passed into the smoking-car.

CHAPTER XII

THE DAWN OF A NEW YEAR

On their arrival at Denver Van and Bob were met by Mr. Blake, and a delay in the train admitted of a passing greeting between Mr. Powers and Van's father; afterward the heavy express that had safely brought the travelers to their journey's end thundered on its way and the boys were left on the platform. Mr. Blake regarded each of them keenly for a moment before speaking; then he extended his hand to Bob, saying:

"The highest compliment I can pay you, young man, is to tell you you are like your father. Mrs. Blake and I are very grateful to you for what you've done for our son."

"I'm afraid--" protested Bob.

Mr. Blake cut him short.

"There, there, we won't discuss it," said he. "I simply wish you to know that both of us have appreciated your friendship for Van. He is a scatter-brained young dog, but he is all we have, and we believe in time he is going to make good. Eh, son?" Despite the words he smiled down at the lad kindly.

"I hope so, Father."

"With a wise friend at your elbow it will be your own fault if you do not," his father declared.

Summoning a porter to carry the luggage the trio followed him to the train which was to take them to the small town outside of Denver, where the Blakes resided.

Here they found Van's mother--very beautiful and very young, it seemed to Bob; a woman of soft voice and pretty southern manner who seemed always to appear in a different gown and many floating scarfs and ribbons. Bob felt at a glance that she would not be the sort of person to pack boxes of goodies and send to her boy; she would always be too busy to do that. That she was, nevertheless, genuinely fond of Van there could be not the smallest doubt, and she welcomed both boys to the great stone house with true Virginian hospitality.

To describe that western sojourn would be a book in itself.

Bob wrote home to his parents volumes about his good times, and still left half the wonders of his Colorado visit untold. There was the trip up Pike's Peak; a two days' jaunt to a gold mine; a horseback ride to a large beet farm in an adjoining town; three weeks of real mountain camping, the joy of which was enhanced by the capture of a good sized bear. In addition to all this there were several fishing trips, and toward the close of the holiday a tour to the Grand Canyon.

It was a never-to-be-forgotten vacation crowded with experiences novel and delightful.

"I wonder, Van, how you can ever be content to leave all this behind and come East to school," remarked Bob to his chum when toward the last of September they once more boarded the train and turned their faces toward Colversham.

"Oh, you see, Dad was born in the East, and he wanted me to have an eastern education," explained Van. "He laughs at himself for the idea though, and says it is only a sentimental notion, as he is convinced a western school would do exactly as well. He has lived out here twenty years now, and yet he still has a tender spot in his heart for New England. It is in his blood, he declares, and he can't get it out. Notwithstanding his love for the East, however, Mother and I say that wild horses couldn't drag him back there to live."

"I suppose you wouldn't want to come East, either," Bob said.

"Not on your life! Give me lots of hustle and plenty of room!" replied Van emphatically. "But I like the East and the eastern people, and I'll be almighty tickled to get back to Colversham and the fellows--to say nothing of Tim McGrew."

"You'll take up football again this fall, of course," said Bob. "We'll both duff right in with the practice squad as soon as the boys get out; it seems to me there is no earthly reason why each of us shouldn't land somewhere on the eleven this year."

Weeks afterward Bob thought with a grim smile of the remark.

How different that fall term proved to be from anything he had expected!

Colversham was reached without disaster and back into the chaos of trunks, suit-cases, and swarming arrivals came the western travelers. From morning until night a stream of boys crossed and recrossed the campus and the air was merry with such characteristic greetings as:

"Ah, there, Blakie! How is the old scout?"

"Snappy work, Bob Carlton! I say, you look pretty kippie. Where did you swipe the yellow shoes?"

"Just wearing them temporarily until I can step into yours as stroke of the crew!" called back Bob good-naturedly.

A shout went up from the boys who had heard the sally.

For nearly a week the school grounds were a-hum with voices. Then things began to settle down into the regular yearly routine. In spite of the stiff program ahead Van managed to spend some part of each day, if only a few moments of it, with Tim McGrew. How much there was to tell! Three months had worked marvels in the little fellow and it was a pleasure to see how his strength was returning.

"The doctor thinks there's a chance I may walk yet, Mr. Blake!" exclaimed the child. "He doesn't promise it, mind; he just says maybe things won't turn out as bad as we thought at first. I heard him tell Ma that perhaps later if I was to be operated on maybe I'd pull through and surprise everybody. Think of it! Think what it means to know there is even a chance. Wouldn't it be wonderful if I should walk again some time?"

Catching the glow in the wistful face Van's own beamed.

"You'll have us all fooled yet, Tim," he cried, "and be prancing round here like a young Kentucky colt--see if you don't."

The lads chuckled together.

Van was bubbling over with high spirits when he left Tim that afternoon and there was nothing to herald the approach of the calamity that fell like a thunderbolt upon him. It was late at night when the illness developed that so alarmed Bob Carlton that it sent him rushing to the telephone to call up the head master. From that moment on things moved with appalling rapidity. Van was carried from the dormitory to the school hospital and at the doctor's advice Mr. Carlton was summoned from New York by telephone. Within an incredibly few hours both he and his wife arrived by motor, and their first act was to wire Van's father.

The boy was very ill, so ill that in an operation lay the one slender chance of saving his life. The case could brook no delay. There was not sufficient time to consult Van's father, or learn from him his preferences as to what should be done. To Mr. Carlton fell the entire responsibility of taking command of the perilous situation. He it was who secured the famous surgeon from New York; who sent for nurses and doctors; who made the decision that meant life or death to the boy who lay suffering on the cot in that silent room.

How leaden were the hours while the lad's existence trembled in the balance!

Mr. Carlton paced the floor of the tiny office, his hands clinched behind him and his lips tightly set. If Van did not survive his would be the word that had sent him to his end. Should the worst befall how should he ever greet that desperate father who was even now hurrying eastward with all the speed that money could purchase? What should he say? What could he say, Mr. Carlton asked himself. To lose his own child would be a grief overwhelming enough; but to have given the order that hurried another man's only boy into eternity-- that would be a tragedy that nothing could ever make right.

"I have done the best I knew," muttered Mr. Carlton over and over to himself. "I have done toward his son precisely as I would have done toward my own. Had I it all to decide over again I could do nothing different."

Yet try as he would to comfort himself the hours before he could have tidings from the operating room dragged with torturing slowness. Bob, crouched in a chair in the corner of the room, dared not speak to his father. Never had he seen him so unnerved. There was no need to question the seriousness of the moment; it brooded in the tenseness of the atmosphere, in the speed with which his heart beat, in the drawn face of the man who never ceased his measured tread up and down the narrow room.

And when the strain of the operation was actually over there was no lessening of anxiety, because for days following the battle for life had still to be waged. Would human strength hold through the combat? That was the question that filled the weary hours of the day and the sleepless watches of the night.

Mr. Carlton, ordinarily so bound up in business affairs that he never could leave town, now gave not a thought to them. Instead he took up his abode in the dormitory with Bob that he might be close at hand, and here he eagerly checked off the successive hours that brought nearer that man who was racing against

Fate across the vast breadth of the country.

How would they meet, these two who had been so long divided by a gulf of years and bitterness? Would his former friend feel that the decisions he had made were wise, or would he heap reproaches upon him for putting in jeopardy a life over which he had no jurisdiction? With dread Mr. Carlton strove to put the thought of the coming interview out of his mind.

"I have done as well as I knew," he reiterated. "Would that it had been my own boy instead of his!"

Over and over he planned to himself what he would say at that crucial meeting. He would explain as nearly as he could the precise conditions that he felt justified him in assuming the immense financial responsibilities he had heaped up for his former friend. If the lad lived it would be worth it all; but if he did not it would all have gone for naught. Would not any father rather have had his child alive, invalid though he was, than to have lost him altogether?

The meeting when it came was quite different from anything Mr. Carlton had outlined. It was after midnight when the special arrived at the dim little station, and even before the train came to a stop its solitary passenger sprang impatiently to the platform.

There was no need for James Carlton to make certain who it was; every line of the form was familiar. He strode to the traveler's side.

The hands of the two men shot out and met in a firm clasp.

"The boy?"

"He is alive, Asa."

"God bless you, Jim!"

Van Blake faced the great crisis, fought his way courageously through it, and won.

Slowly he retraced his steps up the path to health again, and as soon as he was able to be moved he and his father and mother together with the Carltons went to Allenville and opened the old farmhouse for Christmas.

What a Christmas it was!

What a day of rejoicing and thanksgiving among young and old!

Tim McGrew and all his family were brought down for a holiday, and there was a royal tree decked with candles and loaded with gifts; there was a pudding which could nowhere have been matched; a southern plum-pudding made by Van's mother; there were carols sung as only those to whom they meant much could sing them; and there was joy and peace in every heart.

"Next summer it must be Colorado for you all, Jim," cried Asa Blake as he stood with his hand on the shoulder of his old partner. "We'll make this New Year the happiest of our lives. Tim shall go too; and if money can buy surgical skill he shall make the journey hither on his own two feet. Here's to the new year, Jim!"

"The new year, Asa, and may God bless us every one!" echoed Mr. Carlton, softly.

THE END